FIFTH-CENTURY
ATHENS
DEMOCRACY & CITY STATE

ARTS: A SECOND LEVEL COURSE

The Open
University

BLOCK 1
INTRODUCTION TO THE COURSE

**PREPARED FOR THE COURSE TEAM BY
CHRIS EMLYN-JONES AND LORNA HARDWICK**

BLOCK 2
THE GREEK THEATRE IN ITS
DRAMATIC AND SOCIAL
CONTEXT

**(with detailed study of Aeschylus'
Prometheus Bound and *The Persians,* and
Sophocles' *Antigone* and *Oedipus the King*)**

**PREPARED FOR THE COURSE TEAM BY
CHRIS EMLYN-JONES AND JOHN PURKIS**

THE OPEN UNIVERSITY

The Open University
Walton Hall, Milton Keynes
MK7 6AA

First published 1996

Edited, designed and typeset by The Open University.

Printed in The United Kingdom by Page Bros, Norwich.

ISBN 0 7492 1177 6

This text is a component of the Open University course A209 *Fifth-century Athens: Democracy and City State*. Details of this and other Open University courses are available from Course Enquiries Data Service, PO Box 625, Dane Rd, Milton Keynes MK1 1TY; telephone: + 44 - (0)1908 858585.

1.1

13520B/a209b1and2i1.1

BLOCK 1

**INTRODUCTION TO THE
COURSE**

PREPARED FOR THE COURSE TEAM BY
CHRIS EMLYN-JONES AND LORNA HARDWICK

BLOCK 1: CONTENTS

PREFACE TO BLOCK 1

This introductory block is divided into two parts:

This introductory block is divided into two parts:

Part 1 (Sections 1–4)

This part will aim to put fifth-century Athens in its context by considering some basic concepts through guided reading of the set book, *The World of Athens* (Sections 1 and 3). There will be consideration of different categories of evidence (Section 2), and an introduction to methods of analysis on audio-cassette (Section 4).

Part 2 (Sections 5–10)

This will (a) focus on the historical events of the first half of the fifth century and (b) identify themes and topics which will be of continuing importance for the whole course. The use of *The World of Athens* and primary sources will be continued and extended.

In order to study this block you will need:

The World of Athens (WA)

Course Guide (for the maps it contains)

Supplementary Texts (*ST*)

Illustration Booklet I

Audio-cassette 1 (for Band 1) and the associated Audio-cassette Notes

Aeschylus' *The Persians*

Herodotus' *The Histories*, tr. G. Rawlinson (Dent, 1992)

The Offprints

Appendix 1, at the end of Block 2, contains an outline map of the Eastern Mediterranean showing places mentioned in Block 1.

Please note that the bulk of the work in this block comes in the second part, so you should plan to complete Part 1 about half-way through your first week of study, allowing one and a half weeks for Part 2.

PART 1

Prepared for the course team by Chris Emlyn-Jones

1 APPROACHES TO FIFTH-CENTURY ATHENS

1.1 The study of a society

Imagine for a moment that you are a complete outsider about to embark on a study of contemporary British society. Where would you start? What types of question would you ask and what sort of evidence would you look for? Think about this for a moment.

Discussion _____

The obvious place to start would be with individuals: how do the people you are planning to study live, where do they come from, what do they do, how do they govern themselves? But you would probably very soon want to ask questions which took you beyond this to larger structures: for example, the relation of individual, family and government to the class structure, the economy or the legal system. You would then need to ask a third set of questions about the attitudes of individuals and groups; to understand these you would have to inquire into the society's values, which would take you into the role of mass media, education, religion and the arts. And you would need to compare all this with how things look on paper – formal structures of government and administration. Your inquiry could be extended back in time – indeed ultimately it would need to be – in order to look at your findings as part of a historical process of development and change.

The kind of evidence you would look for would depend partly on what type of question you were asking. It would, however, include a mass of basic records, statistics and concrete evidence such as buildings, housing-estates, towns. There would also be available a wealth of evidence based on analyses produced by sociologists, economists, historians and, in a very different sense of the word 'analysis', by novelists, dramatists, artists and poets. ♦

In transferring our attention from our own society to fifth-century Athens, from the familiar to the unfamiliar, there is a strong tendency to assimilate what is strange to what we know: to ask roughly the same questions and expect to find the same kind of evidence – in other words, to carry preconceptions based on our own social and cultural experience into our study of Athenian society. If we do this, we shall continually encounter problems and oddities. For example, an obvious area of interest for us might be Athenian domestic life, how the Athenian family lived and functioned. But research into this will quickly reveal two important facts: firstly that there is an almost complete absence of the kind of evidence we would take for granted in the modern context, such as records of births, marriages and deaths, and domestic accounts. Even the physical remains of domestic housing are relatively scarce.

The second point we will swiftly discover is that classical Greek does not have a word for 'family' as we would now understand it, which implies, to go no further, that we need to consider whether the Athenian social structure contained anything corresponding to the modern idea. To take a further

7

example, we might ask the question: what role did organized religion play in Athenian society? Our curiosity is understandable; but, in direct contrast to the previous example, when we look for evidence we find it almost everywhere, which suggests that the question needs recasting to fit a social phenomenon vastly different from what we would now understand by 'organized religion'.

The conclusion of my argument in this section is not negative: it is one of the main purposes of this course to offer a challenge to preconceptions about Athenian culture – to show that we may need to ask different questions from those that immediately come to mind and to look for evidence in (to us) odd places.

1.2 Images of classical Greece

So, what is the evidence and how do we come by it?

When you decided to take this course, you probably already had some image or idea about what classical Greece was like.

I would like you briefly to write down two or three of the popular images of ancient Greece which immediately came to your mind.

Discussion _____

Among a wide variety, some of the more obvious which occur to me are: sea, sun and ouzo, columned temples, bronze and stone statues of humans (or gods) and dramatic performances in Greek theatres. (Travel brochures and realizations of Greek drama on TV play their part here.) You may also have in your mind less concrete aspects, for example, democracy or even proverbially 'classical' qualities such as elegance and restraint. ♦

In the previous sub-section, we emphasized the importance of our own preconceptions about Athenian society, based upon our own social experience. It is also important to be aware, right at the outset, of the extent to which popular images, and others not so popular, come down to us with the cultural associations of our own *past*. The study of any society, whether it is remote or near in time and place, demands constant awareness of what unconscious cultural assumptions we make today.

Of course, our assumed familiarity with our own past has its own pitfalls; it is not necessarily true that the further a culture is historically from our own, the more difficult it is to interpret. Our own perceptions are, whether we like it or not, closely bound up in all aspects of life with our inheritance from, say, the Victorians, while our sheer distance, historically, from classical Athens (two and a half millenia) and apparent cultural remoteness may help us to be more objective. Yet it is important to recognize that even in this latter case we are heirs to a wealth of cultural attitudes. From the Romans to the Victorians, Greece has regularly featured as a cultural ideal, a model of excellence – hence the 'classical' label. Artists and architects in particular have selected from their source, and have projected backwards on to it, all the admirable and desirable qualities they wished to see in their own culture (see Figures 1–4 for examples).

Nowadays we tend to lay special emphasis on the dangers of assuming that the Greeks were quite like us (or even as we would like to be). The poet Louis Macneice, himself a university Classics teacher for a time in Birmingham in the 1930s, puts it thus (talking about his own teaching experience):

> How one can imagine oneself among them I do not know;
> It was all so unimaginably different
> And all so long ago.

(*Autumn Journal* IX, 77–80)

Figure 1 *Alexander and the family of Darius after the battle of Issus* by A. Bellucci (1654–1726). Painted in a similar style to Figure 3, but on this occasion depicting a historical event from Alexander the Great's conquest of the Persian Empire and defeat of King Dareios (Darius) (333 BCE/BC: see *WA*, p.54).

(Ashmolean Museum, Oxford.)

Figure 2 Downing College, Cambridge, by William Wilkins (1807). A 'Greek' architectural facade.

(Photo: Copyright Country Life Limited.)

Figure 3 *The Judgement of Hercules* by P. de Matteis (1662–1728). The Greek demigod Herakles (Hercules) chooses between Virtue and Vice: an 'image' of a Greek legend in a contemporary classical style.

(Ashmolean Museum, Oxford.)

Figure 4 *Hylas and the Nymphs* (1896) by J.W. Waterhouse (1849–1917).

(City of Manchester Art Gallery.)

In my emphasis, in this sub-section and the last, on the dangers of creating a reflection of our own society in the Greeks, you may have got the impression that I would associate myself with what Macneice says here. If so, this is an impression I would wish to dispel. Without the possibility of some kind of imaginative link between us and the Greeks, you would probably not have chosen to study this course, and I certainly would not have contributed to the writing of it. We need to be aware of the positive aspects of both sides of the argument: to accept the culture of the Athenians as part of our intellectual and social 'roots' (which implies that we can never be totally objective – if objectivity is even theoretically possible) and at the same time to be critically vigilant in recognizing vital differences between us and them.

2   THE NATURE OF THE EVIDENCE

2.1   Types of evidence

The basis of all our critical investigation, the building blocks, as it were, with which we have to work, are the various types of evidence. It is by studying these critically that we are able to construct a coherent and sound historical picture. This may seem quite self-evident; nevertheless I would like to spend a few minutes looking at some of the implications of what I have just said.

At this point, take your set book The World of Athens (WA) *and read Chapter 4, paragraphs 4.1–4.11 (pp.153–7). I am not so much concerned yet with the information these pages convey to you, but I would like you to ask yourself while reading:*

a)   *What is the form in which this book is providing you with information?*

b)   *How might this form relate to what I mentioned in the first paragraph of this section, above?*

Discussion _____

a)   In these paragraphs *WA* provides information organized by topics, proceeding smoothly from one subject to the next, with a plentiful supply of statistics (including two tables).

b)   There is little sign of the evidence I was talking about in the first paragraph of this section! Reading *WA*, you may have received the initial impression that our knowledge of Athens is a smooth and continuous plateau of established fact fitting naturally into this kind of narrative form. In reality, nothing could be further from the truth: in *WA* the sources of evidence for the statements so confidently made have been largely predigested for ease of reference and assimilation. The original terrain or bed-rock on which the plateau rests is extremely uneven. So what you are reading in *WA* is the *end-product* of the scholarly process of interpretation.   ◆

What does fifth-century Athens look like if we go behind WA? *Turn to* WA *Chapter 4 again, and just glance quickly through pages 153–95. What types of evidence can you find? (Look at text and illustrations.)*

Discussion _____

The chapter contains the following evidence:

1   *Written texts.* As I said, *WA* does not normally supply evidence for its statements (if it did, the book would run to several thousand pages and be unreadable into the bargain!). However, note – for example on pp.158, 163 and 165 – that the authors of *WA* quote from written texts in order to illustrate a point. If you look at pages 406–7 of *WA*, you will find an 'Index of Passages Quoted' including all the written sources appearing in the book and where they are quoted. If you then cross-reference some of the names you find

there with the Glossary (*WA*, pp.360–73), you will get an idea of the range of literary sources available, including works by historians, dramatists, philosophers and medical and legal writers.

2   *Inscriptional.* Inscriptions are writing which is inscribed on stone, metal, clay or other material. This type of source is not particularly easy to spot from *WA* Chapter 4, so don't be too discouraged if you missed it; an example is on p.159. You may think this evidence, since it is writing, should be categorized under (1) above. In practice it is more helpful to think of it as a separate category, since inscriptional material comes down to us in a very different form from other types of written text (as you will discover in Section 2.2 below) and fulfils a very different function: inscriptions are mostly the record of public events, decrees, laws, etc. Note that *WA*'s Index has a short section on inscriptions (p.407), quoted from the most accessible modern collections (see also *WA* 'Notes' at the front of the book, p.ix, note 4).

3   *Archaeological.* This source of evidence covers a very wide range, from the remains of whole cities and religious sanctuaries to small art-objects and artefacts. Note that in *WA* Chapter 4, painted pottery appears very prominently in the illustrations. This is partly because of the subject of the chapter: scenes depicted on pots are valuable evidence for different aspects of Athenian social life; but also partly because painted pottery is a plentiful source of evidence in that it has survived in comparatively large quantities. If you glance through the illustrations in other chapters of *WA*, you will see that pottery predominates there too.   ♦

2.2   Survival of evidence

In Sub-section 1.2 we were concerned with the large historical gap between us and fifth-century Athens. But we also have to reckon with the closely related problem of severely limited survival of evidence. This will be immediately obvious in the case of an archaeological site. (You may have noticed when leafing through *WA* Chapter 4 that fifth-century Athenian houses are shown only in drawn reconstruction: p.167; this is because no domestic house survives above its foundations.) Less obvious, but equally important, is the situation with regard to written texts: their authors wrote on a perishable material (papyrus), so survival of their texts has depended on continual recopying and retention in Greek and Roman libraries and medieval monasteries.

Not only does limited survival of the remains of a culture mean large gaps in our knowledge, but it also implies that what does survive needs interpretation. A fifth-century Athenian site may be overlaid with later Greek and Roman, not to mention medieval, building. The reconstruction of the house I mentioned a moment ago (*WA* p.167) depends upon interpretation of the significance of foundations, comparison with other examples elsewhere, and so on. Interpretation is also needed when the copying and recopying of an ancient text over centuries leads to major or minor discrepancies between different manuscripts of the same work, or gaps in the text caused by accidental loss (see Figures 5–8).

2.3   Primary and secondary sources

Before we go further, we need to make a clear distinction, which will be familiar to students who have recently taken the Arts Level 1 Course, between primary and secondary sources. So far, in talking about evidence, what I have been referring to as 'evidence' are primary sources which date from the period for which we are considering evidence – the 'raw material' of the course – whereas secondary sources are later users and interpreters of this material.

Figure 5 (left) Foundations of a private house, west of the Areopagus, Athens. It is from this kind of evidence that architectural reconstructions must be attempted.

(American School of Classical Studies at Athens: Agora Excavations.)

Figure 6 (right) A third-century CE/AD papyrus text of Antiphon the Sophist (fifth-century BCE/BC; an author discussed in Block 5). Note that the poor state of preservation leaves gaps in the text and, in this particular case, there is no other source.

(Cambridge University Library MS Add 6355. Oxyrhynchus Papyri XI no. 1364.)

Figure 7 (left) A papyrus text of Homer's *Iliad*, dating from the first century CE/AD. Clearly visible here are the vertical and horizontal fibres of the plant which, when stuck together, constitute the writing surface.

(Bodleian Library MS Gr. class a.1(P)10.)

Figure 8 (right) A tenth-century CE/AD manuscript of Homer's *Iliad*. Note that the text is surrounded by marginal comments; these are known as scholia.

(Biblioteca Marciana MS gr. 454 fol.41 recto. Photo: Foto Toso, Venice.)

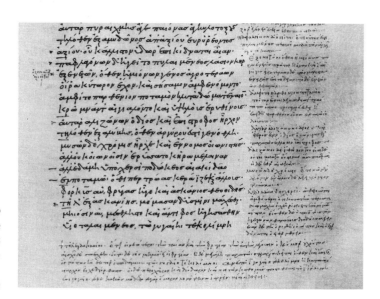

The sources you will encounter in this course can be divided into the following categories:

Ancient

1   Sources roughly contemporary with the period of the course (i.e. during the fifth century, shortly before it, or shortly after it).

2   Sources dating from considerably later than the period being studied but still categorized as ancient sources (i.e. up to about the end of the Roman Empire – fourth and fifth centuries CE/AD).

Modern

3   Sources using categories 1 and 2 for purposes of synthesis (e.g. *WA*), analysis and interpretation.

If you now try to fit these categories into the primary/secondary division which I mentioned at the beginning of this section, you will see that while the functions of 1 and 3 are clear, category 2 occupies an ambiguous position between them; sources in category 2, while technically 'secondary' (i.e. they date from well after the period in question), may sometimes be considered as *interpretative* of earlier material and sometimes they may serve a similar function to category 1 – as raw material for later (that is modern) interpretation. For example, Plutarch – a Greek historian writing in the second century CE/AD – is, despite his distance from fifth-century Athens, the oldest source for certain aspects of the period and must in this respect be treated, with due caution, as a primary source. In most studies of ancient Greece my categories 1 and 2 (ancient sources) are conventionally considered as primary, and category 3 (modern sources) as secondary. This will suffice at this stage, since further explanation will be made at appropriate points in the course; but please bear in mind the distinctions made above.

2.4   Academic authority

If our primary task in this course is to interpret the evidence of ancient sources, how are we to view modern sources which do the same thing? If you look once again at *WA*'s Index (p.407), you will see that amid the ancient sources there is an entry 'Vickers, B. *Towards Greek Tragedy*'. It is very important to grasp the difference in function between this source and the others. Vickers represents the *end-product* of the interpretative process. His function is to do what we are planning to attempt – the construction of argument based upon a critical analysis of evidence. *Your use of Vickers and other category 3 sources is a supplement to critical investigation of sources, not a substitute for it.* I am not saying that the evidence of the most stupid ancient commentator is automatically to be accorded greater credence than the most perspicacious of modern scholars. But if you accept uncritically what modern scholars say, however convincing they sound or however eminent they may be, you are not only undermining the whole purpose of this course but will quite often find yourself at an impasse, since many of the most interesting and important questions about fifth-century Athens not only fail to provide a 'yes or no' answer but are themselves still the object of genuine dispute between experts.

The function of secondary (i.e. category 3) sources, then, is to stimulate ideas, to enable us to see from what evidence arguments are derived and to follow them *critically.* The introduction to The Offprints gives help with critical reading of modern academic writing, and you should refer to it before working on individual articles in The Offprints.

ADDED TO A BOOK ETC.
TO PROVIDE FURTHER
INFORMATION

3 ATHENIAN SOCIETY: SOME BASIC CONCEPTS

In the next three sub-sections we are going to take an initial look at three basic areas, the first two of which form the subtitle of this course: democracy and city-state. We are going to use sections of *WA* as a basis.

3.1 The *polis* (city-state)

At this point please read WA *Chapter 1, pp.62–88, a description of the physical environment of the* polis. *As you read, consider how you might answer the following questions:*

1 *How does the Greek* polis *differ from a modern conception of a city? (Polis is explained in* WA *1.3 as 'a settlement and its surrounding territory'.)*

2 *Athens is clearly seen as an exceptional* polis *in the Greek world. What factors does* WA *suggest may have contributed to this?*

Please read through Chapter 1 now, and then return to the discussion.

Discussion _____

1 a) The first point I would make is that the *polis* was politically independent. In 1.1 and 1.2, *WA* points out that Greeks shared a common culture, but there was no central government. The idea of a self-governing city is one with which you may not be familiar: city-states don't exist in the modern world, except for anomalies such as the Vatican or Monaco, though Venice in the fourteenth and fifteenth centuries has similarities. It may have struck you also that the buildings and functions described in 1.31–7 seem appropriate to a national government.

b) As you were reading through the chapter, it will have become obvious that 'city' does not adequately translate *polis* – which is why we need to use the Greek word. The *polis* of Athens was the whole of its territory, which comprised not only the settlement of Athens (i.e. the area surrounded by its walls) but also a number of other settlements and a large area of land (known as Attica; see Map 3 at the front of *WA*), about the size of an English county or (as *WA* 1.17) the state of Luxembourg.

c) *Polis* also has a range of meanings which does not correspond to those of 'city'. Besides the definition given in *WA* 1.3, *polis* can mean the area surrounded by the city walls, which is what the 'traveller' means in 1.25, when he says 'He then comes to the city of the Athenians' (see also Figure 1.10 on the opposite page in *WA*). It was into the *polis* that people and property from outlying districts of Attica came for shelter behind the walls when the Spartans invaded Attica at the beginning of the Peloponnesian War, as we are told by the historian Thucydides (set book: Book 2.14 ff.).

2 a) The obvious factor contributing to Athens' exceptional nature, *WA* suggests (1.3), is its size (the size of its *whole* territory, not just of the city). 1.10–13 emphasize the overwhelming importance of farming for the *polis*: a large surrounding territory usually meant more cultivable land. Given that their area did not have naturally rich soil, Attica's farmers concentrated on cultivating a crop appropriate to this (1.20).

b) Athens was rich in natural resources, especially metals and stone. Note (1.19) that silver, mined in Attica, was a very important factor in Athenian military power in the fifth century (you will be learning more about this).

c) Athens developed trade to an exceptional degree through its port, the Piraeus (1.23–4), importing commodities which it could not produce locally, chiefly grain. ◆

Before we leave this sub-section, I would like to return to the definition of polis *we looked at in point 1 above. Please look up* polis *in the* WA *Glossary (p.370). Can you find there any aspect of the word I have not dealt with?*

Discussion _____

I mentioned government briefly in point 1(a). But note the emphasis in the *WA Glossary* on citizenship, festivals, customs. In *WA* 1.33 the officers of state take an oath to abide by the state's laws; here 'state' (*polis*) is not really felt as a geographical entity so much as a community of people defined by commitment to certain cultural and political values. In a speech which you will be studying in some detail in Block 4, a funeral speech over the Athenian war-dead, the statesman Pericles says of Athens: '...I say that as a city (*polis*) we are the school of Hellas...' (Thucydides 2.41). Here *polis* encompasses all that we have mentioned so far, but with the addition of patriotism and civic pride. And it was allegiance to the *polis* and not to Greece.   ♦

3.2 Democracy

Unlike 'city-state', the other term of the course's subtitle, 'democracy', is one we use all the time in our own political context. When you hear it said that the Greeks invented democracy, you may think that you know what is meant. But like *polis*, *demokratia* is a word which has its own particular associations, and in this sub-section we aim to become clearer about some of these.

At this point, I would like you to read further in WA. *Before you go on to Block 2, you will need to have read* WA *4.1–36 and 5.1–43 (besides sections from Chapter 2 which I will specify below in Sub-section 3.3). This is quite a lot of reading. You can do it now if you have time in hand; if you are hard-pressed, I suggest you read in a moment 4.1–16 and 5.9–25 (I will be concentrating on material in these sections) and the rest before you begin Part 2 of this block.*

Please read now 4.1–16 and 5.9–25. While doing so, I would like you to cast your mind back to the exercise you did right at the beginning of this introductory block when you considered how you would analyse a society. What aspects of the WA description strike you as differing radically from assumptions you might make about your own society? (I have in mind two major points relevant to Chapter 4 and one to Chapter 5.)

Discussion _____

Chapter 4

1 4.1–11 describe the basic groups which made up the population of Athens. Our experience of the complexity and fluidity of modern socio-economic groupings surely leaves us unprepared for the apparently rigid categories – explicitly defined in clear social and economic terms – which affect the total relationship, political, social and cultural, which the individual person had to the *polis*. In particular, citizenship is clearly a restricted and privileged status in ways totally unlike a modern concept of citizenship.

2 4.12–16 deal with the 'household' (*oikos*). My remarks in Sub-section 1.1 may have prepared you for differences here. Note that *oikos* includes what we would understand by 'family' but implies much more in two respects:

a) *Oikos* is broader and includes not only what we would understand by 'extended family' but also property (land and buildings) and slaves (who were a kind of property).

b) The *oikos* was important to the Athenians in ways much more basic than implied in, for example, modern calls to 'maintain the integrity of the family'. The *oikos* was not only the basis of economic survival, but (quite as important) it was, as *WA* 4. 13 makes clear, the basis of social and political status, the key to citizenship and so to political office. Hence the importance of 'legitimacy and property' – the subheading which follows at 4.17.

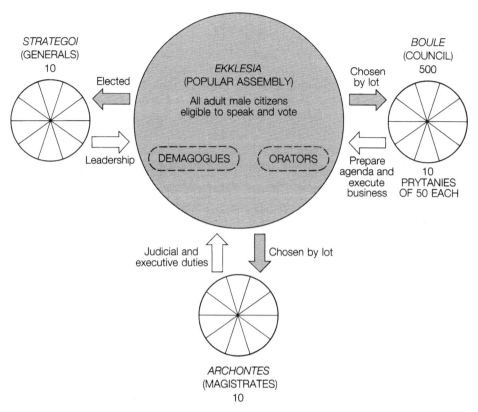

Figure 9 A schematic diagram of the structure of Athenian democracy. This diagram should be studied in conjunction with *WA* 5.9–38.

Chapter 5

The key point is actually spelled out by *WA* at 5.9; Athenian *demokratia* involved direct participation by all adult male citizens (though do bear in mind what you learned in 4.1–11 about the exclusive nature of citizenship). All citizens had the right to speak and vote in the *ekklesia* (citizen assembly) and, through the *boule* (deliberative council), could involve themselves in the day-to-day running of the *polis*. The *boule* was open to all citizens, chosen through their tribes by *lot*, not vote. *WA* 5.26–40 indicate further offices, most of which were filled in the same manner. ◆

3.3 Religion

Please now turn to WA Chapter 2, and read it all through quite quickly (i.e. grasping general points but not worrying too much about detail; if you are short of time, please read at least 2.40–52, though you will need to read the whole chapter before you begin Block 2). While reading, ask yourself: what are the main differences between religion as you understand it in a modern context and what you learn from this chapter about religion in fifth-century Athens?

Discussion

a) The main difference is concerned with function, as I have already strongly hinted in 1.1 above. There is no block solely on religion in this course (although Block 5 considers the late fifth-century 'religious crisis' in the light of philosophical and scientific developments). This is because worship of the gods and religious cult was a function of all aspects of life, public and private (for the latter, see *WA* 2.33). The 'gods of the *polis*' were worshipped at important festivals which marked the passing of the official year (*WA* 2.41–3); large and important temples were dedicated to them; they were a focal point in drama (as we shall see, gods were actually sometimes represented on stage); and the drama itself was part of a festival to the god Dionysos (2.46).

b) Unlike most modern religions (and certainly Christianity), Greek religion had no canonical text or sacred book. The nature and activities of gods and aspects of their relationship with mortals were preserved in a vast and amorphous body of myth (*WA* 2.11). There was no class of professional priests. Both of these facts gave scope for comparative freedom in the interpretation of mythical tradition, about which you will learn much in Block 2.

c) There is a lot in *WA* Chapter 2 about communication between gods and humans (2.8–39). The nature of the relationship between the two groups was crucial because the attitude of the gods to their human worshippers was felt to underlie the prosperity of the *polis* and the individual. Where Athenian conceptions diverge radically from those of the modern era is in how they conceived their gods: they regarded them as inscrutable and liable to be fickle. Most methods of communication involved interpretation (2.13–20) and sacrifice or appeasement (2.28–37). The gods' benevolence could not (to say the least) be taken for granted, and yet their support was vital.

d) The nature of the gods and their behaviour to mortals provides, in many respects, the most radical divergence from most modern religions and so is, perhaps, the most difficult to grasp. On the whole, gods did not, in their conduct, exemplify patterns of behaviour which mortals were expected to follow, but demonstrated their great and, it often seemed, arbitrarily exercised power. Religion was not always a comfort (though note 2.53–5 on Mystery Religion). But the immense power attributed to the gods made it a total necessity. ◆

4   SOURCES AND METHODS (AN AUDIO-CASSETTE EXERCISE)

At this point, having covered some basic points, we are going to conclude the first part of Block 1 by beginning work on the source material by means of an audio-cassette exercise. This exercise aims to start you off with a step-by-step approach to some examples of different types of source which will form a basis for the exercises which you will encounter in Part 2 of this block.

INTERACTIVE

Please have Cassette 1, Band 1 ready for play, with the related Audio-cassette Notes, and switch on when you are ready. You should only return to this block when you have finished Cassette 1, Band 1.

PART 2

Prepared for the course team by Lorna Hardwick

INTRODUCTION TO PART 2

In Part 2 we are going to focus on the historical events of the first half of the fifth century. The work is divided into five main sections:

5   the causes and results of the wars fought between Greeks and Persians in the first part of the fifth century;

6   primary sources: this section includes an extended exercise linking Sections 5 and 7;

7   the role of the Athenians in this conflict and especially their enhanced sense of identity and importance;

8   relations between Greeks and Persians in the fifth century;

9   events between the Persian Wars (when Greeks fought Persians) and the Peloponnesian War (431–404) when Greeks fought Greeks. In this context we shall consider especially the development from a Greek alliance into an Athenian naval empire and the associated tensions between Greek states.

We shall have two principal aims. The first is to gain familiarity with the main events affecting Athens and to establish an outline chronology. The second aim is to identify themes and topics which will be of continuing importance for the whole course. We shall start by using a secondary text, your set book *The World of Athens*, but then we shall move on to using primary sources from the Supplementary Texts and Illustration Booklet I. You will also need to refer to the maps in *WA* and the Course Guide. When we get to Section 6, you may find it useful to refer back to the exercises and discussion on Audio-cassette 1, Band 1, but otherwise no additional cassette work is required. Remember that you can use the outline map in Appendix 1 – at the end of Block 2 – to locate places mentioned in Part 2.

Critical use of *WA*

At this point – now that you have worked through the audio-cassette exercises on sources and methods – you should have achieved a clear sense of the difference between the ancient sources and a modern work such as *WA*, which uses the ancient evidence but does not in general discuss it *critically*. Rather, *WA* aims to present a clear overview or synthesis of the main events and cultural features of ancient Athens.

We can now pause to look more closely and critically at one short section in *WA*. Our aim is to dig beneath the smooth narrative in order to identify some of the types of source that the authors might have used, and to ask some questions about the balance between historical narrative and historical judgements which the authors have achieved.

Please turn to the historical introduction in WA Section 13 (H.I.13: pp.11–12). This is an account of the battle of Marathon (490), a crucial event in the first defeat of the Persians. Read the account carefully several times; then write short notes in response to these questions:

(a) In the first paragraph of the account, how many types of ancient sources of evidence can you identify which might have been used by the authors?

(b) In the second paragraph, pick out any words or phrases that suggest to you that the authors have introduced their own interpretations or judgements.

Discussion _____

(a) First paragraph: how many sources?

'burned': this could be based on documentary evidence from an ancient account and/or on evidence from archaeology. (By examining stones and other burned remains, archaeologists can make judgements about the causes of destruction.)

'convenient landing place': a statement based on documentary evidence and/or topography. (For an illustration outlining evidence from topography, see Figure 10 on p.22.) When citing evidence from topography, it is important to distinguish between ancient sites/landscapes and modern ones; the latter may have changed because of erosion, climatic and/or soil changes.

'make the decision' assumes documentary evidence.

'the generals ... decided' also assumes documentary evidence, perhaps a literary account, although the names of the generals might be got from public inscriptions (*ST* 13e contains a relevant passage from the Greek historian, Herodotus).

Further points: you might have picked out for yourself other phrases such as 'they sent a message to Sparta' and 'forced to delay by religious scruple', which the authors of *WA* derived from ancient narratives about the incident. (They probably used mainly Herodotus 6.102ff., which you can locate in your set text, *The Histories.*) Notice, too, how *both* archaeological and documentary sources are important to even a simple account such as this.

(b) Second paragraph: authors' judgements

You should have noticed 'exotic swashbuckler' as applied to Miltiades. This phrase may be based on descriptions of him in the ancient sources (see, for example, Herodotus 6.104), but there is an element of judgement too (whether from ancient or modern historians). The phrase perhaps also serves to attract the reader's interest!

The sentence 'It was a famous victory' is probably deliberately ambiguous. 'The remarkable achievement of the Athenians' also contains an element of judgement. Notice how the authors indicate the importance of 'song and painting' in the on-going celebration of the victory. In relation to 'song', you will shortly be reading one example, Aeschylus' play *The Persians*; while in painting the battle was commemorated in the murals of the Stoa Poikile in Athens (*poikile*, 'many-hued'). However, even that victory could outstay its welcome: the comic dramatist Aristophanes, writing some sixty years later, mocks – perhaps affectionately – the (by then) elderly 'men of Marathon' with their old soldiers' stories. This shows that the label remained an emotive one.

Now look briefly at the article by G.E.M de Ste Croix in the Offprints. At this stage you are *not* asked to read it but just to look at the first two or three pages where there are footnotes giving details of ancient and modern works that the author has consulted (others are mentioned in the body of the article). Clearly the style and purpose of the article are very different from those of the authors of *WA*.

This does not mean that one is intrinsically better than the other, merely that they are very different examples of modern (secondary) scholarship. Both come into the category of modern/secondary sources described in Sub-section 2.3 above. However, they differ in their functions and the nature of their authority (see Section 2.4 above). The *WA* passage gives us an immediate overview but, since it does not have a scholarly apparatus of references, we are not immediately able to check the sources of the judgements. This means that while *WA* remains a useful introduction to the shape of events in the fifth century, and enables us to 'situate' individuals and groups as well as to identify key issues, we have to investigate the evidence used by the authors in order to be able to formulate our own judgements.   ◆

5   CAUSES AND RESULTS OF THE PERSIAN WARS

5.1   Study strategy

Your set reading is *WA* H.I.12–25, but first some advice on how to approach it. Remember that this is a secondary account which the authors have put together on the basis of judgements they have made about the evidence provided by a number of primary sources. We shall be looking at some of these primary sources later in the block.

In using the material in *WA*, you need to make sure you have grasped the contents both chronologically and geographically. So it is important that you:

1   Make your own rough time-chart of the main events. When you have finished your reading, fill in the events you consider the most important on to the chronological chart in the Course Guide.

2   Locate the places mentioned in *WA* H.I.12–25 on the maps. The full-page map at the back of this book shows the most important places mentioned. Map 5 in *WA* (the Near East and the Persian Empire) provides a broader context (the maps in *WA* are placed after p.xii.). Map 1 in *WA* (the Mediterranean) gives an idea of proportion; Map 1 in the Course Guide gives more detail.

5.2   Interrogating the texts

In reading *WA* we need to be critical. I will be suggesting ways of bringing out important themes and problems in the *WA* text, but your own individual response also has an important role. As you read, consider what questions you would want to ask of the authors' account. For example, where reasons for action are given, can you think of others which might be considered? Never be afraid to ask the obvious question. This independent thought is the first step on the way to critical use of the text. Of course, in order to try to answer the questions you pose, you will want to refer to the ancient evidence; and later in the block (Section 6) we shall be taking the first steps in analysis of some of the primary evidence on which the account in *WA* is based. However, in one introductory block we are obviously not going to get to grips with all the questions that spring into your mind. Some of them will be taken up in detail later in the course. Others are difficult to answer because we lack the necessary evidence. So do regard the paragraphs discussing 'Further questions' as very much open-ended. In the exercises and discussion I will differentiate between these *further (open) questions* and the more *specific questions* to which we can give detailed attention at this stage in the course.

So far as WA H.I.12–25 are concerned, I suggest that as you read (or, if you prefer, on second reading) you make short notes in answer to the following specific questions, which I will then pick up in discussion.

1   *According to the authors of WA, what were the main causes of the Persian Wars?*

2   *What are we told about the extent to which the Greek* poleis *co-operated and how the war effort was organized?*

3   *Is there a suggestion that Athens had a special role? If so, of what kind?*

4   *What were the tangible effects of the Persian Wars?*

Now please read WA H.I. 12–25. (Remember to keep a check on the chronology of events.)

Discussion

1 According to the authors of **WA**, *what were the main causes of the Persian Wars?*

Perhaps we should distinguish between *general* and *specific* causes. For example, you might have said that the narrative shows that the wars (like most wars) were caused by competition for power or disputes over territory. The *specific* cause, however, appears to have been the events leading to the revolt in 499 of the Ionian cities on the coast of Asia Minor. (These cities had been founded by Greeks, some as early as the ninth century.) The Greeks in the Ionian cities were reacting against Persian domination of the coastal area following the expansion westwards of the Persian Empire.

We therefore have a triangular relationship between Greeks (in Greece), Greeks (in Asia Minor) and Persians. This was potentially complex, and in the context of the Ionian revolt there are two points of special note. Firstly, the revolt originated in Miletos where the Persians had installed a tyrant (this information is not in *WA*). The basic characteristic of tyranny is rule by one person, so installation of a tyrant inevitably left a discontented aristocracy excluded from power (see further *WA* H.I.7). Therefore revolt against Persian domination may also imply a power struggle among the Greeks in the Ionian cities. (Herodotus has much to say on this subject.)

Secondly, although the Ionian cities were Greek foundations, relations with other Greek *poleis* seem rather uncertain. Sparta refused help, and although Athens (which was supposed to have long-standing links with the Ionians) did send ships, it may have been as much to guard against the return of the exiled Athenian tyrant Hippias (who was thought to be seeking Persian help) as to help the Ionians. This relationship between struggle for power *within a polis* and its external links with other *poleis* or with Persia will be a pervading theme in the course.

After the collapse of the Ionian revolt in 494, the way was open for the Persian Emperor Dareios to direct his attention further west. This brought Persia into direct conflict with Greek mainland states, notably Athens and Sparta, and in fact conflicts with Persia dominated the politics of the Eastern Mediterranean until the middle of the fifth century.

2 What are we told about how the Greeks fought and about how the war effort was organized?

In looking at the way in which the wars with Persia were conducted, it is difficult to speak of 'the Greeks' in general. You saw from *WA* H.I.12 that initial opposition to Persian expansion had come from Sparta, which by 500 BCE/BC was leader of an alliance of Peloponnesian states and was the most powerful land force in Greece. Nevertheless, the initial land-battle in mainland Greece was actually fought by the Athenians together with the Plataians. The victory at Marathon (490) proved to be a major influence on the direction taken in domestic and inter-state politics, and we shall be looking later in the block at the way it was used in Athenian history and propaganda. Marathon was, however, only the prelude to a series of engagements by land and sea in 480–479 (see *WA* H.I.16). Notice that the Athenians were developing their navy, but that overall command rested with the Spartans. There are some indications that the alliance between the two *poleis* was uneasy (*WA* H.I.19) and that Persia realized it was in its interest to divide them.

Marathon and Salamis (480) were to figure prominently in Athenian propaganda (see Figures 10 and 11 for site maps), but you can tell from the account in *WA* that Plataia (479) was crucial and that Thermopylai, Artemision, and Mykale are also mentioned. Fighting in Asia Minor, Egypt and Cyprus continued until mid-century (*WA* H.I.25) although it was at a safer distance from the Greek mainland. *WA* Chapter 6, 'Athens at War', contains more detailed information about methods of warfare on land and sea, although it should be noted that much of the discussion relates to the fourth century. (If this subject interests you, look at 6.1–6.8, 6.17 and 6.19. However, this is entirely optional.)

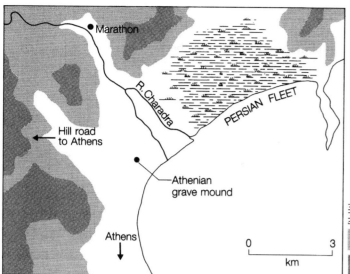
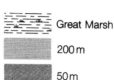

Figure 10 The battle of Marathon, 490 BCE/BC.
The Athenian camp was by the western foothills but the site has not been definitely confirmed. The site of the actual battle is thought to have been west of the River Charadra, confirmed by the site of the Athenian grave mound. Many of the fleeing Persians were thought to have been killed in the area of the Great Marsh.

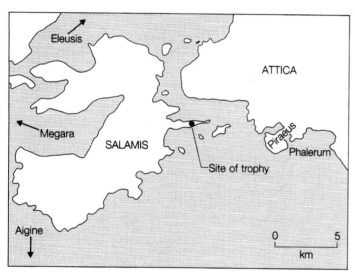

Figure 11 The battle of Salamis, 480 BCE/BC.
The battle took place in the straits between Salamis and Attica but its actual position in the channel is disputed. A battle monument was erected on the Kynosoura promontory.

The other important point to keep in mind at this stage is that Athens was actually twice evacuated (before Salamis and again before Plataia in 479) and was sacked by the Persians (*WA* H.I.18–19).

You might be wondering about the effects on Athens of the Persian invasion of Attica and destruction of the city, and on the Greeks in general of their successful, if sporadic, combination against Persia. These major themes will be taken up later in the course.

3   Is there a suggestion that Athens had a special role? If so, of what kind?

The 'special' role of Athens is a rather slippery topic. You might want to ask: *was* its role really crucial? The points which stand out are its initial involvement with the Ionians, its victories at Marathon and Salamis, its gradual development of sea-power and the fact that its experience of Persian occupation was profound. Yet all these factors take on 'special' status by virtue of the interpretation put on them afterwards, mainly by Athens itself. This therefore brings us on to the fourth of the questions with which we began.

4   What were the tangible effects of the Persian Wars?

These are the main points which you should have gained from *WA*.

a)   Persian expansion westwards was stopped. But Persia remained a powerful force in Asia Minor, and was a factor to be reckoned with in political relations between the Greek states, and sometimes even within states.

b) A significant number of Greek *poleis* had co-operated to ward off the common danger from Persia. Loose alliances between states had been consolidated and new ones formed. Thus the pattern of relationships between the Greek states was changing. Note especially the meeting on the island of Delos in 478–7 when Athens and the allies agreed to co-operate against Persia (*WA* H.I.23).

c) Athens had emerged to take its place alongside Sparta as a leading state of mainland Greece and a strong influence with the islands (*WA* H.I.23–4).

d) The importance of sea-power had been shown and Athens had made significant developments in this respect. ◆

Further (open) questions

1 By now you should certainly be asking yourself: how do we know that the succinct and plausible narrative in *WA* is a reliable account? Can we accept what it says about the details of negotiation and especially about the motives of the various *poleis*?

2 *WA* tends to speak rather generally of 'the Greeks', yet the details of the narrative indicate that individual states took the initiative at different times and places. So we need to ask whether the Greeks really were as united as might be imagined.

3 The Greeks, whether we see them as united or as separate but allied states, had undoubtedly gained an outstanding victory over superior numbers. The effect of this on future policy, and on *intangibles* such as attitudes, needs to be studied.

(Questions 2 and 3 above may not have occurred to you but Question 1 certainly should.)

The purpose of Section 6, which follows, is to suggest ways of beginning to answer these questions.

6 PRIMARY SOURCES

We have to turn to primary sources in order to clarify our response to Questions 1 and 2 set out above. Keep in mind Question 3 also, because the matter of *attitude* to the threat posed by Persia and to the victories won does, of course, affect the way in which the ancient sources present their evidence.

Below is a list of the sources we are going to use. They represent a broad cross-section of the kind of primary evidence used by the authors of *WA* to make their synthesis. For each, I shall want you first to think about the information about the source given in the Supplementary Texts, the nature and purpose of the source, when it was produced, by and for whom. Then consider especially whether it bears on *what happened* or on *attitudes* towards what happened (or both). Does it throw up further problems?

This exercise builds on your experience of working on Cassette 1, Band 1, which you studied with Part 1 of this block. If for any reason you have not worked through the band, you should do so now before proceeding.

Then, and only then, will you be in a position to step back from the source and decide whether it broadly supports the account given in *WA*, or whether it suggests a different emphasis or a significantly different perspective.

The cassette exercises on sources are an *essential* part of your learning and will help you to develop skills which later blocks of this course will assume that you have mastered.

To aid the discussion, I have grouped the sources by type into commemorative, literary, and historical narrative. I suggest you look at each group as I come to it in the discussion, following the procedure I have outlined above and taking account of any additional suggestions or reading guidelines I include.

Primary sources

1   *WA* illustration H.I.8. The Athenian burial mound at Marathon.

2   *WA* illustration H.I.13. Athene reading a list of Athenian dead (cf. Illustration Booklet I, Plate I.64).

3   Illustration Booklet I, Plate I.43. Extract from the south frieze of the temple of Athene Nike on the Acropolis (Greeks against Persians).

4   *ST* 17 (a), (i) and (ii). Athenian dedications at Delphi (*re* Marathon and Salamis).

5   *ST* 17 (a), (iii). Inscription on serpent pedestal at Delphi (and cf. *WA* illustration H.I.11).

6   *ST* 22 (a) (b) and (c), Pindar: *Pythian 1*, lines 75–80; *Isthmian 5*, lines 48–53 (Aeginetans and Salamis); Fragment 76 (Athens as bulwark of Greece).

7   Aeschylus, *The Persians*, in Penguin Classics edition of *Prometheus Bound* (trans. Vellacott). From entry of Messenger, lines 250ff. (p.130) to end of Chorus, line 594 (p.139).

8   *ST* 13 (a) (d) (e) (g) (i) (j) (k), Herodotus: *The Histories*, Bk 1.1, 6.102–3, 109, 7.144, 8. 41, 8.52–3, 8.142–4. (At this stage, I suggest that for ease of reference you consult Herodotus in *ST* where the extracts are collected together for you.)

6.1   Commemorative sources

First, study those sources which are broadly commemorative. Look at nos 1, 2, 3, 4 and 5 from my list.

Discussion _____

The Athenian burial mound at Marathon (no. 1) testifies to the Athenian sense of the magnitude of the victory. Historians are not in total agreement about whether at this time it was usual or unusual to bury soldiers where they fell. Later in the century, their bodies were usually cremated and the ashes returned to their families. There was then a corporate civic funeral (the Funeral Speech in Thucydides 2.36–46, *WA* p.56, claims to record such an occasion). However, the nature and siting of this monument suggest, I think, that the Athenians intended it as a visible sign for other Greeks. The Athenian dedications at Delphi (no. 4) similarly indicate a desire to record the extent of their achievement for public consumption at a sacred site used by *all* the Greeks. (Notice that Marathon is specifically named.)

Figure 12 Base with the Marathon Epigrams.
The inscription is from a fragment of the base of a memorial erected in Athens to the dead of Marathon. Restoration of this piece together with another fragment and a fourth-century copy indicates that the text probably read:

> The courage of these men will shine forever as a permanent light
> To those whom the gods may in future grant success in deeds of war
> For on foot and in fast sailing ships
> They kept all Greece from seeing a day of slavery.

(American School of Classical Studies at Athens: Agora Excavations.)

According to Herodotus (9.81), tithes of the booty gained from the defeat of the Persians were given for Apollo at Delphi, Zeus at Olympia and Poseidon at the Isthmus. From Apollo's share was dedicated a tripod which stood on a bronze pedestal formed of three entwined serpents. *WA* illustration H.I.11 depicts the remains. Notice that on the inscription (no. 5) giving the names of Greek *poleis* which fought in the war, Sparta's name is first. This is because the Spartans ordered the inscription. Thus we see both Sparta and Athens promoting their own roles, but in the context of dedications at a site sacred for all the Greeks. The inscription, although incomplete, also gives some indication of the cooperative war effort from many states.

I would therefore say that these three sources of evidence (nos 1, 4, 5) broadly support the account given in *WA*, although they should also draw our attention to the way that victory was perceived and presented at the time.

The marble relief *stele* (c.460–450) (no. 2) is commonly known as the Mourning Athene. I have included it here partly because of the interest of the pose and military equipment (helmet and spear), but mainly to question the caption in *WA*. The relief does not in fact show that she is 'reading a casualty list' (and given the perspective *could* not show exactly what is inscribed on the stone she is looking at). The attribution is pure speculation and, even if she is mourning (which seems possible from the pose, although she could merely be resting), there is no way of knowing whether the object of the mourning is an individual or a group/collective.

The Nike frieze (no. 3) (dating from the late fifth century, although commissioned in the 430s) is interesting because it breaks from the usual mythological subject-matter of such reliefs to show what appears to be a historical event. This has been interpreted as Greeks fighting Persians. Perhaps this is an indication of the almost mythological status that the Persian Wars had begun to assume by the second half of the century so that it was no longer considered

Figure 13 Tridrachm of Delphi.

The coin was found in Egypt. Its value was three drachmas and it may have been struck from silver captured after the battle of Plataia in 479.

Two rams' heads are depicted and above their heads are two dolphins. There is thus a double allusion to Apollo to whom the ram was sacred and who was said to have arrived at Delphi on a dolphin.

(From Assiut, Egypt. Diameter 31 mm. Weight 18.51 gm. British Museum 1971.5–13.1. Reproduced by permission of the Trustees of the British Museum.)

an insult to the gods for sculpture to depict humans performing heroic acts. In Block 4 you will be looking in detail at the genesis and subject-matter of the new building on the Acropolis. The column blocks of the old Parthenon destroyed by the Persians were embedded in the side of the Acropolis. At this stage the main points to note are that the subject-matter of the frieze was considered appropriate for a temple dedicated to Athene Nike (Athene goddess of victory) and that a historical victory had begun to assume mythological status. ♦

6.2 Literary sources

Next please look at no. 6 in my list, the extracts from the Odes of Pindar printed in ST 22.

Discussion _____

I am always slightly averse to 'fishing' in short extracts from literary texts in order to make historical points. It is normally essential to establish first the overall structure within which the poet or dramatist is using language. Later in the course we shall be confronting the problems of methodology this raises for the historian. Here, however, I am asking you to focus only on a very limited area of *content*. These are extracts from commissioned poems, written by a non-Athenian to celebrate athletic victories and the honour obtained for the victor's own *polis*. Notice the way the poet concentrates on praise of the city of his patron and especially the almost cynical assumption in *Pythian 1* that it is appropriate to write of Salamis for an Athenian patron (or an Aeginetan: see *Isthmian 5*) and of Plataia for a Spartan. ♦

So far, from these sources I think we can infer that defeat of Persia was not primarily or necessarily thought of as victory by 'the Greeks'. There is quite strong evidence on a number of these sources that the fragmented nature of the campaign was recognized and that each city sought to identify and promote its own role.

Bearing this in mind, I would like you next to study a longer extract, from a play by Aeschylus, *The Persians*, produced in 472 BCE/BC, eight years after the battle of Salamis. Two points about the play are of special interest. It is the only extant example (apart from comedy) of a Greek play which reworks not mythology but history (and recent history at that); and the *choregos* (financer and producer, see *WA* 5.71) was Pericles, then an ambitious young politician. The play is included in the Penguin edition with another Aeschylus set text, *Prometheus Bound*. Set in the palace of Xerxes at Susa during the aftermath of Salamis, it contains a marvellous creation in words, not only of the extremities of the sea-battle, but also of the cataclysmic impact of disaster.

Later, you will read The Persians *in its entirety, but at this point please read from the Messenger's Speech (line 250, p.130) up to the end of the Chorus at line 594, p.139. As you read, make short notes in response to the questions on the following page:*

1   *How is the role of the Athenians presented? What attention is given to other Greek states?*

2   *How is the Persian loss characterized? In other words, what have the Persians lost and how does Aeschylus convey this?*

Discussion

1   *How is the role of the Athenians presented? What attention is given to other Greek states?*

As we might expect, in a production for an Athenian festival, the role of Athens is pre-eminent. Although the attention is focused on Salamis, there is mention of Marathon (line 291). The (Persian) Messenger's comments emphasize that not only is Athens favoured by the gods (line 347) but that its strength is in its *citizens*:

> ATOSSA: Is Athens then not ravaged after all?

> MESSENGER: While she has men, a city's bulwarks stand unmoved.

These lines (348–9) neatly bypass the horrors of the burning and destruction to which Athens was twice subject.

Figure 14 Seal of Dareios.

A cylinder seal of agate depicting the king hunting lion from a chariot. Palm trees provide a framework. An inscription at the side is in Old Persian, Elamite and Babylonian cuneiform: 'I, Dareios, the King'. This probably refers to Dareios the First (521–485).

(From Thebes, Egypt. Sixth–fifth century. Height 3.7 cm. British Museum 89132. Reproduced by permission of the Trustees of the British Museum.)

Figure 15 Titles of Xerxes.
Part of a trilingual cuneiform inscription from the Persian capital, Persepolis. The full inscription includes reference to 'Xerxes, the great king, the King of Kings, the King of countries having many [kinds of] human beings, the king of this great earth far and wide, the son of Dareios the king'.

(From Persepolis. Fifth century. Height 35 cm. British Museum 118841. Reproduced by permission of the Trustees of the British Museum.)

There is also some emphasis on the communal interests of the Greeks, by a rhetorical appeal to ancestral tombs, temples, etc. (for example, lines 400ff.). Later in the play the ghost of Dareios evokes the Spartan victory at Plataia, but the overall tone presents the Athenians as the champions of these interests.

2   How is the Persian loss characterized?

Did you notice the Messenger's emphasis on the exploits of individual Persians (lines 302ff.)? The incidents are presented in a way remarkably similar to Homer's account, in the *Iliad*, of the fights between Greek and Trojan heroes. (The influence of Homer on Greek literature is discussed in Cassette Lecture 1.) The analogy between epic struggles and those between Greeks and Persians was also taken up later in public sculpture (as you saw when you looked at the Nike frieze). The presentation of the Persian opponents as heroic in stature in a sense elevates the Athenian achievement, but notice that individual Athenians are not singled out by name. The effect is to present victory as a communal achievement.

Another important element is Aeschylus' treatment of the suffering of the defeated (for example, lines 478ff.). There is a fine balance between the emphasis on Persian suffering, which elevates the magnitude of the Athenian victory, and a sensitive communication of the agonies of total defeat. In Block 4 we shall be reading Euripides' *The Women of Troy*, a play written towards the end of the fifth century, in which the sufferings of the defeated are explored in a very different way. In Aeschylus' play, a sense of Athenian triumph is underpinned by the dramatic use of graphic description in the Messenger's speeches, intertwined with poignant lament from the Persian queen, Atossa. The two aspects are brought together in the comment of the chorus at lines 533ff.

When you read the whole of *The Persians*, you will see that Aeschylus also uses the ghost of Dareios to suggest a sense in which the Persian defeat is self-inflicted, the result of their sacrilege in invading the sacred sites in Greece and desecrating temples and shrines. His speech (lines 880ff., p.145) takes up the religious themes explored in the passage you read at lines 400ff.

So in response to our guiding questions, I would say this source does not *directly* support or deny the accuracy of the narrative in *WA*. It draws our attention, however, to the way in which the psychological and ideological implications of victory were explored at Athens. In particular I am not going to get enmeshed in the question about the extent to which the account of the battle is accurate: that is not the main point. We do not look for total accuracy in a dramatic monologue. Mood and symbolic significance are more important. The question of accuracy is taken up by Vellacott in the introduction (p.17). If you read this, notice also how he seems almost carried away by Athenian propaganda! Yet in the end I'd want to argue that *The Persians* is not merely or even primarily a propaganda play. It is true that it represents a stage in the assimilation to historical mythology of a bloody and fragmented series of engagements. However, the dramatic integrity of the play, drawing its force from the suffering and lament of Atossa, brings a degree of dignity and intensity to grief and loss. This rounds out the experience and emotions of wars and defeat rather than merely conveying the triumph of victory.   ♦

6.3   Historical narrative sources

Finally, I want to look at Herodotus. He is the historian of the Persian Wars and you may well be surprised that I have left him until last. The reason is that I wanted you first of all to start thinking about the relationship between *what* we are told and the way it is presented.

Please read carefully the information about Herodotus given in the Introduction to ST 13 in the Supplementary Texts. Then read the very first words with which he opens his account – extract (a) – and then extracts (d), (e), (g), (i), (j) and (k).

Figure 16 Persian 'immortal'.
A glazed brick relief panel from the Palace of Dareios at Susa, *c*.500, depicting one of the 10,000 troops of the Persian Royal Guard, known as the 'immortals'. Herodotus (Book 7.62) describes typical features of the Persian dress as soft felt cap, sleeved tunic, 'fish-scale' mail-coat and trousers. He also describes the arms usually carried as light wicker shield, quiver, spear, bow with cane arrows and dagger carried behind the right thigh.

(From Susa. *c*.500. Height 1.47 m. British Museum 132525. Reproduced by permission of the Trustees of the British Museum.)

Figure 17 Scythian archer.
Bronze statuette of Scythian archer on horseback. The Scythians came from north of the Black Sea and were among Xerxes' troops in the invasion of Greece. Herodotus refers to their caps, trousers and the bows, daggers and battle-axes they carried, and they are depicted in this way on a number of vases.

(From Santa Maria di Capua, Italy. *c*.500. Height 11.5 cm. British Museum WT796. Reproduced by permission of the Trustees of the British Museum.

Discussion

You can see from his opening words that Herodotus attributes as much importance to the Persians ('barbarians') as to the Greeks. This is reflected in the details and balance of the text, and led to his being stigmatized by Plutarch as *philobarbaros* (barbarian-lover). The set passages provide the primary evidence for important aspects of the narrative you have studied in *WA*: for example, the role of Athenian exiles in helping the Persians; the primacy of the Athenian general Miltiades; the dominant role of Themistokles in promoting naval expansion; and the acute danger to Athens itself brought by Persian invasion.

Yet there are also certain problems in using Herodotus as a source. These are concerned with his viewpoint, the influences to which he was subject and the fact that he was writing with full advantage of hindsight. You will have noticed his admiration for Miltiades, a member of a leading Athenian family, the Philaidai. Their rivals, the Alkmaionidai, also figure prominently in his account. Some historians have argued that Herodotus' attitudes were influenced by these powerful figures. In fact, it can be shown that his treatment of them is far from uncritical. Nevertheless it is true that the prominence given to leading individuals and their sources of power inside and outside Athens does emphasize the idea of a Hellenic aristocracy. The apparent hostility of Herodotus to the Athenian democratic leader, Themistokles (for example, in Book 8.5) gives some support to theories that the primary information came to the historian via aristocratic channels.

Perhaps more important for our purposes, since it is reflected in the terminology used in WA, is the way Herodotus tends to think of the Greeks collectively. This is reflected in his emphasis on the ideas of collective freedom, pan-Hellenic religion etc. It is salutary to compare the speech put into the mouths of the Athenians when denying Spartan fears that they are about to make an alliance with Persia (8.144, quoted in WA 1.1) with the presentation of the Athenians in *The Persians* as representative of Greek culture. Compare also Herodotus' views on the decisive role of the Athenians (7.139). Later in this block, I shall be questioning whether the rhetorical use of apparently pan-Hellenic arguments had any real foundation in fact. Certainly Herodotus, because of his knowledge of what happened later, may have given stronger identity to Greek ideas of collective freedom from the barbarian than were current at the time *about which* he wrote (as compared to the time *at which* he wrote), while at 7.139 he is clearly assessing the Athenian contribution to victory in a longer historical perspective.

Finally, we need to take notice of Herodotus' appreciation that the Athenians' initial decision to send ships to the aid of the Ionians set in train a long and eventually disastrous sequence of events. Here is a selection of his comments:

> These ships were the beginning of disaster for both the Greeks and the barbarians.
>
> (5.97, extract (c))

> Greece experienced disasters ... some caused by the Persians, but others caused by rivalry for leadership among those states fighting the war.
>
> (6.98, not in your Supplementary Texts)

See also Herodotus 8.3 for discussion of rivalry between Athens and Sparta. ♦

7 THE ATHENIANS' SENSE OF IDENTITY

Throughout Section 6 we saw some tension between the way in which victory over the Persians was interpreted selectively by individual states and the way in which victory was given even greater status by being portrayed as a triumphant preservation of the freedom of Greeks as a whole from Asian domination. We saw in Herodotus, especially in 7.139 and 8.142–4, that he presented a dual aspect to the status of the Athenians by emphasizing both their essential 'Greekness' *and* their unique role in withstanding Persia.

Look again at Herodotus 8.144 (ST 13(k)) and note down the unifying factors among the Greeks, to which the Athenians refer. Then turn to the extracts from Isokrates' Panegyricus: ST 18(a). *This is a fourth-century political document (published about 380 BCE/BC) in which the author makes a rhetorical appeal for Athenian leadership of Greece in a unifying war against Persia. Read it carefully, noting the justifications put forward by Isokrates. Then compare it with Herodotus' treatment. What is similar? Is there anything different?*

Clearly there are significant differences in purpose and tone between the two works. Isokrates is writing in the early fourth century when Athens was rebuilding its role after defeat in the Peloponnesian War (in which Isokrates grew up). Elsewhere in his writing he records his apology for Athenian conduct during the war between the Greek states, but here when he refers to 'that greatest war' (71) and 'the most famous of our wars' (68) he refers to the Persian Wars. Isokrates is looking back, trying to justify present policy with reference to the past, both historical and mythological. He uses the role of the Athenians in the Persian Wars as a yardstick of greatness. His aim is to persuade the Athenians to reassert the qualities they are said to have shown in the past and to persuade the rest of the Greeks that they should recognize the uniqueness of the Athenians' past achievement as a basis for present policies. His aim is to *persuade*.

In contrast, Herodotus is writing a history. His account of the Athenians' speech purports to *record* the ideas most influential in decision-making during the Persian Wars, while his comment at 7.139 represents his later reflection on the significance of the decisions.

Nevertheless, there is some continuity in the statement of the factors that draw the Greeks together. The Athenians in Herodotus speak of 'our common blood, our common language and the temples of the gods and sacrifices for which we share a common ritual' (8.144) while Isokrates, too, stresses culture and religion as unifying factors among the Greeks.

Both writers confront the question of Athenian leadership. Isokrates does so directly, Herodotus does so obliquely in this passage and with the advantage of hindsight in 7.139. Look especially at the words attributed by Herodotus to the Spartan ambassadors in 8.142: 'Also it would be intolerable if the Athenians, who have always in the past had the reputation of bringing freedom to many men, should now be the cause of the enslavement of the Greeks.' Remember that the context of the debate is the supposed intention of the Athenians to make an agreement with the Persians. The Athenian reply, stressing what is *common* among the Greeks, is intended to be reassuring and should be understood in the context of diplomatic debate rather than as the heady statement of pan-Hellenic ideals with which it is sometimes identified.

Isokrates, reacting to events of the intervening century, states Hellenic cultural unity even more graphically, but as a pillar of the claim of the Athenians to the leadership of Greece. The Athenian claim is based partly on their unique identity, partly on their achievements. Isokrates claims the Athenians are unique because they are the only inhabitants of Greece who are truly indigenous (*Panegyricus* 24). His argument is that they are descended from Mother Earth and have stayed in the same place undisplaced by invasion. (This theme of *autochthony* was used by many orators and poets: see Thucydides 1.2.) Isokrates then claims that, as shown in mythology, the Athenians are the fountainhead of agriculture, the associates of the Greek hero Theseus and the benefactors of minor states through the colonization of Ionia. He says that authority is their due because of their achievements as leaders in the victory over the Persians and especially because of their conduct at Marathon: 'when [the Persians] invaded Attica the Athenians did not wait for their allies, but made the common war their own and set out with a force of their own against those who held the whole of Greece in contempt' (*Panegyricus* 85).

The religious and mythological themes identified by Isokrates had been an important feature of art and literature in the fifth century, and we shall be studying some of them in Block 4, alongside the parallel use made of historical themes from the Persian Wars. Isokrates' articulation of these themes would be understood in the context of public awareness of the political and psychological importance of these ideas. What is important for our concerns in this block is that a sense of Greekness and of Athenian uniqueness are not mutually exclusive. It is the combination of the two ideas which underlies the Athenian justification of its supremacy. This is fully articulated in the fourth-century document by Isokrates, but we can see the contributory points of it in Herodotus and the other primary sources you have studied. In the remaining sections of this block we will look at the political and economic framework within which fifth-century Athenian power developed. (The technical term for the exercise of such leadership/dominance is 'hegemony'.) ♦

8 RELATIONS BETWEEN GREEKS AND PERSIANS IN THE FIFTH CENTURY

This section has two aims. The first is to emphasize how Greek–Persian relations form a significant strand running through fifth-century (and fourth-century) history and culture, i.e. the importance of the Persians (and of Greek perceptions of them) did not simply cease after their defeat by the Greeks in 479.

Look again at H.I.25 in WA and note down on your chronological chart the main events in the continuing struggle between Greeks and Persians during 476–49. Notice the locations and consider who else was involved. What does this pattern suggest?

Discussion _____

We can see a struggle for influence in the whole area of the North Aegean, Asia Minor and the Eastern Mediterranean as far south as Egypt. Sea-power has a significant role, and the operation of the Delian league forces seems to indicate an attempt to reconcile joint action among the Greeks with exploitation of the situation by some individual *poleis* for their own interests. ♦

Later in the course (Block 3) you will be following the development of this situation in the context of the war between Athens (and its allies) and Sparta (and its allies). At the end of the century the role of Persia became crucial to the outcome of the war.

Now read Thucydides' History of the Peloponnesian War, *8.17–18 and 8.28–9, to discover the machinations between Athens, Sparta and the Persian governor in Asia Minor (Tissaphernes) at the end of the fifth century.*

The second aim of the section is to consider two important examples of ways in which the ancient sources treat the relationships between Greeks and Persians.

Herodotus as a source: historical narrative

You will find it useful to read the introduction by Hugh Bowden to your Herodotus set text. Then look at Herodotus 6.102, 107 and 112. What kinds of evidence do the passages offer about how the Greeks regarded the Persians?

Discussion _____

There seem to be two very different kinds of attitude recorded here. The first is shown by the fact that the Persians were allied with some Greeks. Herodotus recounts this in a matter-of-fact way and does not imply that this was exceptional. Furthermore Hippias (the son of the Athenian tyrant Pisistratus), who acted as guide to the Persians (102, 107), presumably saw their victory as a means of restoring political power to his family.

The second kind of attitude is shown in 6.112 where Herodotus writes of the fear that the Greeks felt for the unfamiliar dress and fighting tactics of the Medes (troops in the Persian army). Here, it would be useful to compare your impressions of Herodotus' writing with those of Momigliano in the first three pages of his article in The Offprints. ◆

Notice, especially, Momigliano's comments on the two types of historical research carried out by Herodotus, and his praise of Herodotus as a historian who was knowledgeable about the East. It is particularly important to be aware of Herodotus' use of oral traditions: you may well have noted that these passages in Herodotus make us aware of a complexity of political intrigue, and also convey a sense of cultural identities and differences that the authors of WA, perfectly understandably, omitted from their account of the events surrounding the battle of Marathon. (Herodotus also gives more prominence to the religious context of decision-making and fighting.)

You have already – in Sections 6 and 7 – encountered evidence of how images of Persia and the Persians became a significant force in later Athenian politics and culture. One particularly important source dates from very close to the Greek victory over Persia, and gives a unique and in many ways surprising insight both into attitudes towards that victory and into the working out of much broader cultural processes. That source is Aeschylus' play The Persians.

Aeschylus as a source: drama

Aeschylus' 'The Persians': a preliminary reading

At this stage, I would like you to read the play straight through, pausing only to note any aspects of Aeschylus' depiction of the Persians that strike you as remarkable. In Block 2 you will have the opportunity to study the play in detail as an example of a Greek tragedy and in comparison with other examples of the genre. Please read the play now before returning to my points below.

Aeschylus' depiction of the Persians: staging and language

The first point to be made is that there are no Greeks on stage in the play. Aeschylus is not, for instance, setting out opposition between Greeks and Persians in terms of conflict between different characters in the play. Because the interaction is between different *Persian* individuals and groups (the Chorus of Elders, the Queen Atossa, the ghost of Darius, Xerxes himself), the play allows the exploration of a range of feelings and perspectives. This prevents facile stereotyping of the Persians as a whole. Nevertheless the original production may be assumed to have used costume to represent a Persian ethos: fine linen, tiara, distinctive turban and yellow-dyed slippers are all referred to by the Chorus (ll 660–2). Evidence from vase-painting shows that ethnically differentiated clothing was a feature of visual representation.

Interpretation of Aeschylus' depiction of the Persians is difficult because, inevitably, cultural factors creep in (our own as well as those of the Greeks). For example, the display of emotion in suffering may induce sympathy or contempt, or a mixture of the two. It is perfectly possible that Aeschylus *both* constructs a picture of Persian custom as different from that of the Greeks *and* genuinely engages with the human emotions and situation underlying it.

A close analysis of the language that Aeschylus used has shown that linguistic differentiation plays an important part in his construction of Persian attitudes and values. Notice especially his distinction between the battle-cry of the Greeks (ll 399–404) and the confused shouting of the Persians (l 404). This is linked with the stress on certain kinds of behaviour – for example, Xerxes' cruel threat to behead his naval commanders (l 367), the fear felt by the Persians when they heard the Greeks singing (l 392), the collapse of Persian

33

power when opposed by Greek cunning and intelligence (for example, the false message in ll 355-64) and the contrast between the discipline of the Greeks and the flight of the Persians (ll 374-5, 424). In a detailed study, Edith Hall has pointed out how these images became part of a Greek construction of Persian inferiority (see Hall, 1989 in the Further Reading at the end of this block). In addition, hierarchy, luxury and emotional response are repeatedly shown by Aeschylus to be implicitly in opposition to the qualities that the Athenians admired in themselves (civic democracy, simplicity and control; see, for example, ll 583-94).

In the light of my comments and your own notes, please re-read the Messenger's sequence (ll 353-532) and the Chorus that follows (533-95). Jot down any phrases that are directly relevant to the issues discussed above, taking note also of the discussion in Section 6.2 above.

(When you turn again to the play in Block 2, you will have the opportunity to consider how far it involves propaganda alongside tragic drama. At that time, keep by you the notes you have just made of your first impressions. You should find them useful: close reading of the text underlies all the judgements you will be asked to make.)

Finally, read Herodotus' account of the aftermath of the battle of Salamis (Book 8.93-9). To what extent is his characterization of the Persians compatible with that of Aeschylus? (Again, justify your judgement by referring to specific examples from the texts.)

9   ATHENS FROM PERSIAN TO PELOPONNESIAN WARS

9.1   The *Pentekontaëtia*

(The 50 years from 479-431 are known as the *Pentekontaëtia*.)

These years are covered in WA H.I.22-34. Please read this now, noting down what you consider the most important points under the following headings:

1   Relations between Athens and Sparta.

2   Factors affecting Athenian policy.

3   Relations between Athens and its allies. (Make sure you look up on Map 4 in the Course Guide the places mentioned.)

In the discussion I shall add further information and explanation to the points you find for yourselves in WA. Additions will be in brackets.

Discussion _____

1   Relations between Athens and Sparta

In 478 Sparta was still the leader of the Greek alliance, Pausanias controlling the fleet. However, Spartan leadership was not permanently established, partly because Pausanias antagonized the Greeks in the Hellespont region. The allies in the islands turned to Athens for leadership. Sparta remained as leader of the Peloponnesian league (see Course Guide Map 3). (Herodotus Book 8.3, *ST* 13 (h), says Pausanias' conduct gave the Athenians a *pretext* for taking the leadership. He clearly implies there was rivalry already.)

Sparta objected to the increasing power of Athens, but failed to get Athens to dismantle the walls round Athens and the Piraeus which were being built under the leadership of Themistokles. Sparta's strength was reduced by its anxieties about political stability at home. The Spartans were a minority in their own territory. This is in direct contrast to the confidence and dynamism of the developing Athenian democracy. There seems to have been disagreement in Athens about whether the real enemy was Persia or Sparta. His supposedly pro-Spartan activity led to the ostracism of the Athenian leader Kimon. There was intermittent warfare between Sparta (and its allies) and Athens (and its allies) from about 460–446. (*Direct* conflict between Athens and Sparta occurred only at three points, apart from the battle of Tanagra. In 465 Sparta threatened to invade Athens, the occasion being a dispute over Athenian pressure on Thasos. In 446 Sparta briefly invaded Attica. In 440 Sparta voted to attack Athens because of the latter's treatment of Samos, but was out-voted by its own allies in the Peloponnesian league.)

The relations between Athens and Sparta in these years are summarized in a rather schematic way by Thucydides in Book 1.18–19. (Look up this passage if you wish.) He sees these years as part of a gradual process leading to the major war between the two states, which started in 431, and in Book 1.23 concludes that 'what made war inevitable was the growth of Athenian power and the fear which this caused in Sparta'.

2 Factors affecting Athenian policy

These include the interests pursued, the ways in which the Athenians extended their power, *and* the difficulties and problems which stimulated them to act in certain directions.

Military and Naval

It is in a sense misleading to speak of the 'aftermath of the Persian Wars' (*WA*, p.18). What happened was that the main war effort against Persia moved to Asia Minor and Egypt (H.I.25). Look up the places mentioned and add them with the dates to your chronological chart. The continuing threat from Persia and the need to defend the islands provided a continuing need and justification for the alliance generally known in modern times as the Delian League. The failure of Sparta to provide positive leadership after 478 left the way open for Athens to develop the necessary sea-power to defend the Aegean and the islands.

Economic

Naval requirements coincided with Athenian economic needs. Grain shipments from south Russia via the Black Sea were important. Athens also had to ensure the availability of timber for its growing fleet. Thrace was an important source (see Course Guide Maps 2 and 3). In spite of the primacy of Laureion as a source of precious metal, back-up sources were needed, hence perhaps the conflict over Thasos in 465. Note, however, that Thucydides does not mention these factors: he attributes Athenian leadership rather to a desire to extract revenge and booty from the Persians (Book 1.96).

Political

The Athenian decision to require most of the allies to contribute money rather than ships (*WA* H.I.23) is significant and is perhaps the result of strategic, economic and political considerations. If Athens collected tribute money and then provided the fleet herself, she controlled it in a way which was impossible if ships were provided directly by the allies. The method of provision affected Athens' relationship with the allied states (see below) but there were also implications at home, notably in ensuring the availability of funds for a vast programme of public works and in fostering an ideology in the democracy which was both civic and imperialist. The use of communal rather than private funding permitted a level of naval and civic expenditure which could not have been sustained by the wealthy citizens alone. This marks a key turning point in the move away from the political dominance by aristocratic families. This theme will be taken up in Block 4.

3 Relations between Athens and its allies

The overall picture is of the development by the Athenians from leadership of a voluntary alliance into domination of an empire.

Notice especially the hint (in *WA* H.I.25) that the initiatives taken by the Athenians promoted their own advantage and that this was perceived as just as important as threatening Persia (perhaps even more so). Force was brought to bear on allies threatening to withdraw from the Delian League (H.I.26) and most of the allies contributed money rather than ships. (There may have been political and social reasons why the allies too preferred this method.) The great power of Athens was naval, and its mid-century attempt to extend to a land-empire was frustrated by Sparta (H.I.32).   ◆

9.2   From Alliance to Empire

It is important to realize that the features of imperialism did not emerge all at once. Particular events and trends can be explained more clearly by competition between Athens and Sparta and by the need for Athens to protect its interests against both Sparta and Persia, than by claims that Athens intended from the beginning to dominate Greece. However, in spite of some undoubted advantages in economic prosperity and collective security, there can be no doubt that the developed empire was oppressive and was perceived as such by the subject allies. The most important means of control were:

a) The use of imperial institutions and taxes to protect the corn supply to Athens and to safeguard supplies of timber and metals.

b) The use of military and administrative garrisons in the subject states, in conjunction with the Athenian fleet.

c) The hearing of important legal cases in Athenian courts.

d) The use of religious sanctions to promote ideas of Athenian supremacy. You have seen how victories were commemorated in dedications at Pan-Hellenic sites. We also have an inscription dating from the second half of the fifth century which shows that tribute-paying allies were expected to participate in a politicized cult at Athens (see the 'First-fruits to Eleusis' inscription, *ST* 17(e)).

e) The settlement or exploitation of allied or conquered land by Athenians.

f) The use of tribute to finance the fleet, thus directly benefiting the Athenian wealthy classes (who were spared the cost) and the poorer citizens (who rowed the ships and fought in them) as well as ensuring that operational control remained with the Athenians.

g) Interference in the internal politics of the subject allies to ensure a regime (usually but not invariably democratic) which would support Athens.

Needless to say there has been enormous controversy among historians about all these issues, and I have set them out only as a general indication. We shall be looking at Greek attitudes to Empire in more detail when we study Thucydides in Block 3, although much of the ancient evidence is patchy and sometimes difficult to interpret.

A somewhat schematized account of Athenian imperialism and its economics appears in *WA* 5.78–94; it is important for the guidance it gives on the interpretation of evidence from inscriptions. You can *either* read this now, noting down any points you wish to query *or* leave it for fuller study in conjunction with Block 3.

9.3 The Funeral Speech

To conclude this introductory block, please read the extract from the Funeral Speech (attributed to Pericles by Thucydides) which is included in WA, pp.56–61. At this stage it is not necessary to read WA Chapter 3 (as WA recommends) but you should look at Chapter 4, 4.77–8 for information about the place of funerals in the Athenian value system. Note that the occasion is a public one, a funeral for those killed in the first year of the Peloponnesian War.

As you read, pay special attention to the association of military and cultural supremacy and the strong sense of communal values which is portrayed.

Later in the course, we shall be considering the special role of the Funeral Oration as a genre in Greek public propaganda and deciding how we can test the validity of the claims made in this particular speech, but for the moment it is enough if you note the unique role attributed to Athens, the confident celebration of the capabilities of the human spirit, and the association of religious cult with civic values. We have already considered the first of these topics in the historical context of Athenian response to the Persian Wars. The second and third topics underlie the broader-based study of Greek drama which is the subject of the next block.

A final cautionary thought: Thucydides, the recorder of the Funeral Speech, states that a future observer looking at the remains of Athens would overestimate its power, while in the case of Sparta the reverse would be true (Book 1.10).

10 POSTSCRIPT

At the beginning of this part of the block, I said that it contained two principal aims. The first aim was for you to gain familiarity with the main events affecting Athens and to establish an outline chronology. You can check this by deciding how you are going to fill in the chronological chart in the Course Guide. Check also that you are familiar with the key places on the map in Appendix 1. You should by now have grasped the time sequence of the Ionian Revolt and its collapse, and the main Persian–Greek battles of Marathon, Salamis and Plataia. Also, you should now be able to refer to the relevant ancient sources to consider the ways in which the Greeks recorded their achievements for themselves and for posterity and have a general understanding of the way in which the Greek naval alliance came to be dominated by Athens and transformed into an empire.

The second aim was to identify themes and topics which will be of continuing importance for the whole course. This was a more open-ended aim, approached mainly through the Further (Open) Questions which emerged from the more specific questions and discussions. My basic list is quite short and you may have thought of further topics which you would like to raise at a tutorial or day-school:

Hellenism

To what extent did the Greeks co-operate as Greeks rather than as Athenians, Spartans etc. pursuing their own interests?

To what extent did they think of themselves as Greeks? Are there any unifying cultural features we can point to?

Politics

How important is the link between struggle for power within a *polis* and its relationship with the other *poleis*?

Religion

How was this used to *express* social and political values?

Was it used to *influence* policy and behaviour?

Invasion

How did Athens respond to Persian invasion? Were there long-term effects?

Sea power

How and why was this developed? What were the political effects in Greece as a whole and internally in Athens?

Revenue/tribute

What can we discover about how and why the Athenian *polis* used the money it obtained?

Empire/leadership/authority/freedom

What do the sources suggest about the attitude of the Greeks to these?

10.1 Further Reading

If Herodotus interests you, you could look at Books 6–9 in more detail. Book 8 is particularly relevant.

Further Reading on Greeks and Persians

GOLDHILL, S. (1988) 'Battle narrative and politics in Aeschylus' *Persae*', *Journal of Hellenic Studies*, cviii, 189–93.

GOULD, J. (1989) *Herodotus*, London, Weidenfeld and Nicolson (Chapter 6, 'Reading Herodotus', has a helpful discussion on Herodotus as *both* a mid-fifth century thinker *and* a writer in the epic Homeric tradition).

HALL, E. (1989) *Inventing the Barbarian: Greek self-definition through tragedy*, Oxford, Clarendon Press.

HALL, E. (1993) 'Asia unmanned: images of victory in classical Athens' in J. Rich and G. Shipley (eds) *War and Society in the Greek World*, Routledge, pp.108–33.

HALL, E. (ed.) (1995) *Aeschylus: 'The Persians'*, Aris and Phillips.

SHARWOOD-SMITH, J. (1990) *Greece and the Persians*, Bristol Classical Press.

The most useful modern treatment of Greek history for you to consult would be S. Hornblower, *The Greek World 479–323 BC* (Methuen, 1983). Chapters 1–3 contain discussion of some of the themes introduced in this block as do Chapters 1–3 of J.K. Davies, *Democracy and Classical Greece* (Fontana, 1978).

Both the Hornblower and Davies books also contain extensive material relevant to the rest of the course.

BLOCK 2

THE GREEK THEATRE IN ITS DRAMATIC AND SOCIAL CONTEXT

(with detailed study of Aeschylus'
Prometheus Bound and *The Persians*, and
Sophocles' *Antigone* and *Oedipus the King*)

PREPARED FOR THE COURSE TEAM BY
CHRIS EMLYN-JONES (Sections 1–3 and 5–6)
AND JOHN PURKIS (Section 4)

BLOCK 2: CONTENTS

PREFACE

Block 2 is the first of the four major blocks in A209. In this block we shall be examining Greek tragedy in its dramatic and social context, through detailed reading of four plays – Aeschylus' *Prometheus Bound* and *The Persians*, and Sophocles' *Antigone* and *Oedipus the King*. Greek drama, as well as being an important artistic creation in its own right, deals also with themes whose treatment raises social, cultural and religious issues. Although this block provides the most detailed examination of Greek tragedy, tragedy and comedy will recur later in the course as an important source of evidence with relevance to a variety of themes.

In this block we shall be emphasizing both the individual dramatic qualities of tragedy and also its wider relevance. Section 1 will deal with the immediate social, cultural and dramatic background: Sections 2–5 (the longest part of the block) will be concerned with a detailed study of the four plays, while Section 6 will widen the context again to consider comparisons and contrasts and the plays' broader significance. There will be *two* TMAs associated with this block (for details, see the Study Calendar).

In order to study this block, you will need:

1 Set books

Aeschylus' *Prometheus Bound* and *The Persians*, in *Prometheus Bound and Other Plays*, trans. P. Vellacott (Penguin, 1961).

Sophocles' *Antigone* and *Oedipus the King*, in *The Three Theban Plays*, trans. by R. Fagles (Penguin, 1984).

Please note that line and page references to both these set books are to these translations and do not necessarily match the Greek text or other English versions.

You will also need the Supplementary Texts (ST) and The World of Athens *(WA) for other primary sources and background.*

2 Audio-cassettes

You will need an audio-cassette player for Cassette 1 (Interactive Cassette), Cassettes 6, 7, 11 and 12 (Performance Cassettes) and Cassette 9 (Guest Lectures, Band 1). Also keep the Television and Audio-cassette Notes handy. The purpose of assembling all the audio-cassette material is so that you can study Greek drama not merely as words on a page but also as something which is (as it undoubtedly was) performed. The audio-cassettes will offer:

a) At various points in the block, discussion of questions specifically relating to the dramas as a spoken medium (Interactive Cassette, Cassette 1).

b) A simple performing version of all plays in the set book translation, so that you can read and listen simultaneously (Performance Cassettes: Cassettes 6, 7, 11 and 12).

c) A short 'lecture' by a scholar from outside the Course Team (with Course Team comment) on a topic closely related to the central theme of the block (Lecture 1, on Cassette 9).

Detailed instruction for the use of audio-cassettes will be issued at relevant places in the block.

3 Television

There are three television programmes related to this block:

TV1: '*Seize the Fire*: a modern realization of *Prometheus Bound* by Tom Paulin'. This adaptation was specially commissioned for the course.

TV2: 'The Present in the Past: Authenticity in Greek Drama'

TV3: 'The Theatre and the State: Archaeological Reconstruction'

Television complements the other course material in two ways: by examining tragedy in performance, showing how modern versions of Greek plays and attempts to stage the originals both contribute to a discussion of the problems of *interpreting* them (TVs 1 and 2); and by using the existing remains of ancient Greek theatres as a basis for reconstructing the physical and social context in which the plays were performed (TV3).

For details of programmes and their rationale, please look at the Television and Audio-cassette Notes. The relationship of TV to block discussion will be explained as we go along. As the programmes are available on cassettes, you will be able to view them at your convenience; the study plan below suggests how, ideally, they fit into the work on this block.

4 The Offprints

These are designed to introduce a critical study of modern scholarship. For Block 2 you will require only the first article, by E.R. Dodds, to be read where indicated.

Study plan

We have estimated that all the material in this block is equivalent to five weeks' work. As we explained above, the block is divided into four sections of unequal length. Sections 2–5, the detailed study of the plays, are likely to occupy most of your time. The plan of your five weeks' work might look (on a rough estimate) as follows:

Sections 1–3, with TV1	2 weeks	(TMA 02)
Section 4–5, with TV2	2 weeks	} (TMA 03)
Section 6, with TV3	1 week	

Study pattern

The structure of this block reflects the development of A209 from an original 30-point course (A294). In A294, two plays were studied (Aeschylus' *Prometheus Bound* and Sophocles' *Antigone*); for our 60-point course, the scope of the block has been extended by adding the other two plays. With each playwright, the first play (*Prometheus Bound* and *Antigone*, Sections 2 and 4) is given extended and detailed treatment, while the second (*The Persians* and *Oedipus the King*, Sections 3 and 5) is examined in terms of key topics and issues, with the aim of encouraging you to develop your own ability to apply the skills and techniques learned while studying the earlier play. (This strategy was successfully tested on a group of students doing a pilot version of A209 for credit in 1995.)

This difference in approach should be reflected in your own notes: while it will take you much less time simply to read Sections 3 and 5, you should spend the extra time reading around – and making notes on – some of the questions raised there. (Lines of approach will be clearly indicated in context.)

1 THE BACKGROUND TO THE DRAMATIC PERFORMANCE

1.1 Introduction

In the second part of Block 1, you read through Aeschylus' *The Persians* in a context which emphasized the importance of the play as evidence for the Athenian response to the Persian Wars. The very fact that a Greek play could be used as evidence for a popular attitude should lead you to question ideas about drama derived from our modern conception of the theatre as an exclusive, minority interest. In terms of numbers, popular appeal and emotional involvement, rough modern analogies may be made with spectators at a football match, the audience at a rock concert or the congregation at a papal open-air mass. But neither separately nor together do these modern events really give an adequate idea of the ancient Greek theatrical experience, either in terms of social context or, more particularly, the object of the spectators' attention – the drama itself.

The ancient evidence you will be studying in this block is basically of two kinds: firstly, the plays themselves, and secondly, evidence concerning their context. You will have an opportunity shortly to study the plays in detail; before embarking on this, we are going to examine briefly the physical setting and look at some evidence for the context of the dramatic performance. Unlike the plays, which will provide you with something to get your teeth into, evidence for the background – and, in particular, the social context of the drama – is patchy and sometimes difficult. In the time available to us, you will have to take some details on trust (with the help of WA); however, in order to give you some insight into the nature of the source material, we shall be examining two or three sources for what went on in the theatre before the performance. (Here we are looking mainly at the literary evidence; the important information from detailed investigation of the archaeological remains of theatres *in situ* will later also be brought into the picture: TV3). I shall refer chiefly to tragedy, though some of the details apply equally to the comic drama which took place at the same time.

At this point please read carefully WA 7.35–7.

In what follows, I shall assume that you have the basic knowledge of the background to Greek tragedy contained in these sections of WA.

1.2 The Festival of the City Dionysia

The first point to note is that the popular element in Greek drama, which I mentioned at the beginning of 1.1, derives from its setting – a major Attic religious spring festival lasting a week, in which not only Athenians from outlying areas but non-Athenians would converge on the city. Thucydides, 5.23 (p.362, Penguin), states the terms of the peace of Nikias in 421, which are to involve a renewal of oaths 'by the Spartans [i.e. representatives] going to Athens for the Dionysia and by the Athenians going to Sparta for the Hyacinthia'. Central to the festival was the religious procession which ceremonially installed the wooden image of the god Dionysos in his temple behind the theatre of Dionysos on the south slope of the Acropolis. (The route started at the Academy outside the city wall; see Figure 1:10 (top) in WA, p.79, for the location of the theatre, and Figure 1 overleaf for the site of the temple.) Other elements of the festival included further religious ceremonies, athletic and musical competitions and feasting. It was a major public holiday, during which there was much revelry and drinking, and during which prisoners were even released on bail.

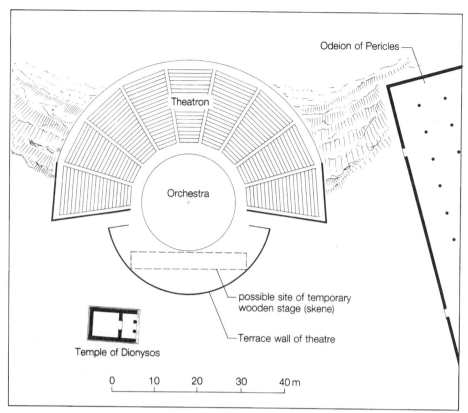

Figure 1 The Theatre of Dionysos at Athens: reconstruction of probable layout in the second half of the fifth century BCE. For more detailed discussion, see TV3 and notes. (Based on J. Travlos, *A Pictorial Dictionary of Athens*, London, Thames and Hudson, 1971, no. 677, p.540.)

1.3 The context of the drama

The religious context of the drama is underlined by its setting within the festival and its physical siting in the theatre of Dionysos; the priest of the god occupied the central seat in the theatre, and an altar to Dionysos was the centrepiece of the large circular *orchestra* (see Figure 1). The performance was preceded by religious ceremonies and sacrifices.

A second aspect of the dramatic performance – which at first sight may not fit easily with the religious element – is the part played by the city in its political guise. The bulk of the audience would have been the citizens who also attended the Assembly and sat as jurors in the Law Courts. However, the citizens were not merely spectators: the whole dramatic festival, like the choral and athletic events, was competitive, and ten citizens from the Athenian tribes would judge between competing playwrights. For tragedy, three playwrights competed with four plays each; for comedy, which was presented also at another Athenian festival, the Lenaia, five plays were presented by different playwrights (see *WA* 7.36). The *choregi* (men appointed to pay for the upkeep and training of the dramatic Chorus, who undertook the task as a *liturgy* – see *WA* 5.71 for an explanation of this word) were chosen by the Eponymous Archon (see *WA* Glossary, *arkhon*) at the start of the year, as were poets and actors. The members of the Chorus were essentially 'amateurs' and were recruited on a tribal basis. *ST* 24(a) provides late, but not necessarily false, evidence that the ten generals were not only habitually involved in the religious sacrifices preceding the drama, but were on one occasion commandeered as judges.

A third factor, associated with the content of the drama but not, as far as we know, integral to the plays themselves, was the effect of the presence of non-Athenians at the gathering. By the time of the Festival, at the end of March, winter was over and land and sea routes open. We have already noted the planned exchange of visits by Spartan and Athenian diplomats in 421; we can

[handwritten margin note: SOMEONE WHO DOES A VOLUNTRY TASK FOR THE COMMUNITY]

6

Figure 2 Theatre of Dionysos, Athens. The remains date chiefly from the Roman period (see TV3) . (Photo: Hannibal.)

assume that further international diplomacy took place, and that diplomats would have attended the dramatic performances, as well as the other events. Clearly, the City Dionysia was an occasion when the city not only provided entertainment for its own citizens but also put itself on show for the Greek world.

To conclude this brief survey, I would like to take this last point a little further in asking you to consider two pieces of evidence related to specific events which, allegedly, played a significant role in the dramatic festival.

Please now read ST 18(b) and 5(a) and consider:

1 *What information they contain concerning what went on in the theatre before the plays were performed.*

2 *What value you would place on the source of information. (For this second question you need to consider the nature of the source: for Isokrates, refer back to the introduction to ST 18(a) and (b); for Aristophanes, see WA Glossary.)*

Discussion (each source is taken in turn) _____

1 The Isokrates passage describes two rituals which, he says, took place in the theatre, when it was full (for the dramatic performance, we may assume). The first of these was designed, according to our source, to emphasize Athens' wealth and prestige as leader of the Empire; the second (an official 'coming of age' ceremony for orphans) to demonstrate Athens' own efforts on behalf of her allies. In considering the value to be placed on this source, it is important to note that Isokrates, a writer of political treatises, lived through the Peloponnesian War but that, in this work, he is looking back seventy years or so; strictly speaking, therefore, he is not in this case a contemporary source. You should also note that he is not merely stating historical facts but displaying a definite attitude of disapproval. In looking back

from the mid-fourth century (the date of the treatise), he is exposing what he now sees as the imperialistic folly of those who waged the Peloponnesian War which he contrasts with the great days of the Persian Wars. (Do you remember encountering this *idée fixe* of Isokrates before in Block 1, Section 7?) We have no idea from this source exactly when these rituals were introduced, although they cannot predate the transfer of the Delian Treasury to Athens in *c.*454 BCE (*WA* H.I.26). Nor do we know how long they were maintained, and we have only Isokrates' word for it that the Athenians were resented because of it.

2 You might note, however, that Isokrates' basic point – the link between the City Dionysia and allies' tribute – seems to be confirmed by *ST* 5(a), an extract from *The Acharnians* (425 BCE), by the comic playwright Aristophanes, who makes his chief character comment that the play is being put on in the Lenaia (a domestic festival, for the Athenians alone, in contrast to the City Dionysia). The absence of 'foreigners' means that he can speak even more freely than usual; he remarks incidentally on the absence of allies and tribute; their implied presence at the Dionysia is confirmed by the scholiast, a later marginal commentator on the text, who also, valuably for us, cites another comic playwright, Eupolis, a contemporary of Aristophanes.

We do not know the details of the ritual nor, most important, how long it was maintained during the latter part of our period; but Aristophanes and Eupolis provide valuable corroborative evidence for the facts, and the presence of tribute in the *orchestra* suggests an important link between the theatre and Athens' imperial role. ◆

Having considered briefly both the value and difficulties of literary source material concerned with the background, we must now move on to examine the dramatic performance in more detail and focus on tragedy itself. (You will be meeting comedy, by Aristophanes, as well as more tragedy, in Blocks 4 and 5.) Meanwhile, I would like you to keep in mind the three aspects of the dramatic context of the City Dionysia which have emerged so far:

1 *The religious*

   The proximity of the temple; the context of the festival; the presence of the priest; libations and sacrifices.

2 *The part played by the* polis

   The participation of citizens and state officials in the competition; the presence and function of elected generals.

3 *The international (Greek and non-Greek)*

   The presence of 'foreigners', ambassadors and allies, bearing in mind the evidence for rituals involving war-orphans and display of tribute. Perhaps we need to add a National Thanksgiving service in Westminster Abbey to our list of analogies in 1.1!

1.4 The tragedians and their works

The question of the origins of tragedy, including the disputed derivation of the word *tragoidia*, is succinctly set out in *WA* 7.37 and I do not want to pursue this here. (If you are interested in this topic, see Section 6.5, Further Reading, at the end of this block.) It is enough to note here that by the time of the Persian Wars (490–79 BCE), tragedy had attained more or less the form in which it continued to be produced throughout the century. This period coincided with the early career of Aeschylus (525–456), the first major tragic dramatist. The last plays of Sophocles (496–406) and Euripides (485–406) are the final tragedies that survive for us (though tragedies continued to be written). So the working lives of these three span our period.

The names of other writers of tragedy are known, but only fragments of their work survive. Even of the three mentioned above, we possess only a small proportion of their full output – 32 plays out of about 300 known by their titles or fragmentary remains (see *WA* 7.36, final paragraph).

In this course you will be reading and studying a number of tragedies chosen partly for their intrinsic quality and interest and partly for the way in which they illuminate the chosen themes of the course as a whole. Yet, even so, it would be impossible to cover adequately the range of themes and treatment even of the surviving plays – a range which, incidentally, demonstrates a much wider conception of 'tragedy' than that implied by the modern usage of the word or even, for example, by the Tragedies of Shakespeare.

Before you go further, please read WA *7.38–40. From your reading of these sections of* WA*, what important points emerge about (1) the subjects of tragedies, and (2) their treatment by individual dramatists?*

Discussion

1 The plots of almost all the tragedies were taken from the accumulated myth and legend that formed the Athenians' conception of their own Greek past.

2 As *WA* demonstrates with examples (7.39), Athenian playwrights had the freedom to exercise their individual creative imagination in treating a particular legend in a variety of ways. The basic story had to remain the same but the details could differ markedly.

This creative freedom has a further implication. As *WA* emphasizes (7.40), plays set in the past also relate implicitly (in varying degrees) to the present – the world of the Athenians' personal and communal experience. So the playwrights have a particular role in interpreting the 'past' (and hence the 'present') for their audience; and, as you saw in the case of the Messenger Speech from Aeschylus' *The Persians* (see Block 1, Section 6.2), this interpretative role of the dramatist can exist even in a play based on events which occurred only a few years before the performance. ◆

During your reading of this block you should listen to Band 1 of Cassette 9, a Guest Lecture by Oliver Taplin on 'Homer and Greek Tragedy'. Although you do not read Homer in this course, his poems are very important as a source and inspiration for Greek tragedy. You may find it best to listen to the audio-cassette when you have studied most of the block.

1.5 Tragedy in its physical setting

In what follows I shall be assuming that you have read and assimilated WA 7.50–52. Please also note that, in this and following sections, I shall be introducing a few technical terms related to the structure of the drama (these are given in Figure 4) and the design of the Greek theatre.

Before you resume reading the block, please look at the second diagram of the Greek theatre (Figure 3) in conjunction with your set text, Prometheus Bound. *Glance briefly at the first few pages of* Prometheus Bound, *including the stage directions, but without reading thoroughly. What initial points occur to you about the structure of the play?*

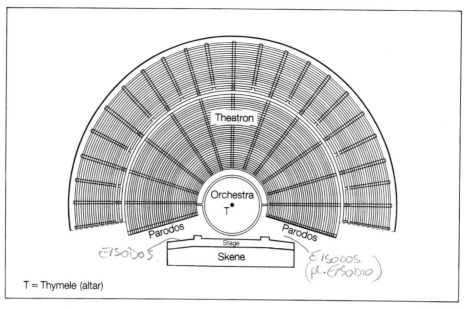

Figure 3 Schematic plan of Greek theatre (based on plan of Epidauros). Look at this in conjunction with Figure 4.

Discussion

The most obvious feature, perhaps, is the way in which there appear to be clear formal divisions between sections of the drama, and formality in the organization of speech within individual sections. This, and the fact that the speech of the play is entirely in poetic metre, distinguishes it from most modern drama, though not of course from Shakespeare or Racine.

A brief survey may also have yielded the following:

1   Speeches and regular dialogue of an argumentative type by and between characters (pp.20–23), accompanied by action (p.22). These are called *episodes* (see Figure 4).

2   'Solo' speech of a more lyrical kind (pp.23–4). The change to different line-lengths for Prometheus' first speech indicates a change of poetic metre in the Greek original.

3   The entry (p.25) of the Chorus (*parodos*: see Figure 4). If you pursue your survey further, you will see that the Chorus, once they have entered, remain 'on stage' until the end (p.52). During the course of the play they have two main functions: they perform at regular intervals a lyric 'passage' on their own (for example, pp.32–3, 36–7, 46–7); this is called a *stasimon*: see Figure 4. They also engage in dialogue with the characters (for example, p.26).   ♦

I have used this brief exercise as an introduction to what will be of major importance in this unit – the need to relate the words of the play which you see on the page to the supposed circumstances of performance in the Greek theatre of the fifth century BCE. As we progress, you will find that there is a great deal that we just do not know about this subject. In this connection it will be important for you to view TV2, which explores different performing styles in the context of 'authenticity'. However, for now, let's briefly consider what we *do* know by further considering three important elements in the drama.

You will need to refer to the Greek theatre diagram (Figure 3) while reading the following sub-section on the details of Greek theatre performance.

A The physical shape of the theatre	
Eisodos (pl. *eisodoi*)	Each of the two side-entrances between the stage and the seats of the theatre.
Mechane	Crane: a mechanical device which could convey an actor through the air.
Orchestra	The large circular dancing area in the centre of the theatre.
Parodos (pl. *parodoi*)	Identical to *eisodos* (above) but also used to refer to the entry-song of the Chorus (see below).
Skene	Literally 'tent'; the stage building and/or stage in front of it.
Theatron	The section of the theatre where the audience sat.
B The plays and their structure	
Chorus	A group of singers and dancers who took on a collective role within a play, performing in the *orchestra*. Also refers to the sections of the play performed by the Chorus.
Episode	Section of a tragedy between the Choral songs.
Exodos	Exit of the Chorus.
Kommos	A lyric exchange between Chorus and actor(s).
Lyric	Used to describe those parts of the drama not in dialogue (i.e. spoken) metre, especially choral songs (odes).
Parodos	The entry-song of the Chorus (but see definition in (A) above).
Stasimon	A choral song (other than the *parodos*).
Stichomythia	Swift exchange of lines between actors (one or two each) in dramatic dialogue.
Strophe/antistrophe	The two complementary matching sections of the choral song (and dance).
Trilogy	Three tragedies with a related theme, performed together.
Tetralogy	Trilogy, with addition of a satyr play.

Figure 4   Some technical terms relating to the Greek theatre

1   The Chorus

The Chorus often seems the most alien and intrusive feature of modern productions of Greek drama, and is certainly difficult to present – as will become obvious to you when you see TVs 1 and 2. Yet for the audience in the ancient theatre, the Chorus was the most visually obvious element of the drama: throughout almost the whole performance, it occupied the focal point of the theatre – the large circular orchestra around which roughly two-thirds of the audience was seated. The first function of the Chorus which we mentioned above was the most prominent: the lyric interlude was sung and danced in the *orchestra* (see Figure 3: the Greek word means 'dancing place'). The metrical form of the words of this *stasimon* (which is all that remains to us of its musical element) is often structurally complex and represents the basis of a spectacle in which music and dancing played a prominent part. Note *WA* 7.37, last sentence: 'Originally Greek tragedy was far more like an opera than what we would call a play.' The complexity of the Chorus' performance is reflected in the great emphasis on training the Chorus (see Section 1.3 above).

2 The characters

The other major focus of the audience was the stage, a narrow platform on the far side of the *orchestra*. Behind this was a simple 'back-stage' changing room whose front wall formed a backdrop for the scene of the play. This was called a *skene*, which means 'tent' or 'hut', from which we derive English 'scene'. The *skene* probably had a single door through which entrances and exits were made. Although a stone structure existed from the late fourth century onwards, it is likely that the fifth-century theatre of Dionysos had a wooden stage, the front of which was raised little, if at all, above the *orchestra*. This was the place from where the actors playing the characters of the play principally spoke (they also used the *orchestra*, although the Chorus never used the stage). The precise nature of this feature of the original theatre is discussed in detail in TV3.

In *Prometheus Bound* there are a number of characters (see p.20 of the set text); however, if you glance briefly through the play, you may notice that, besides the Chorus, there are never more than two speaking characters on stage at any time. (Though four actors are required in the first scene, two of them – Prometheus and Violence – are silent.) If you are reading Greek tragedy for the first time, you may be struck by its 'static' quality in comparison with more familiar dramatic traditions. This is a complex topic, to which we shall return; but one obvious aspect is the restriction on the number of speaking actors taking part in a tragedy, namely two (and later three). The reason for the restriction is hard to determine: it has been explained in terms of the evolution of drama or its religious and ritual aspects or, more mundanely, related to equity (treating all dramatists alike), or expense or scarcity of expertise (unlike the Chorus, actors were paid professionals). However, Peter Walcot (see Section 6.5, Further Reading) rightly warns of the danger of assuming that Greek tragedians necessarily saw the restriction in the number of actors as an artistic limitation.

Delivering speeches and engaging in dialogue were the main functions of characters in the play, but the characters also sometimes took part in the singing and dancing associated with the lyric exchanges of the Chorus.

3 Visual elements

a) Action

No ancient text of Greek drama, as far as we know, contained any stage directions (*WA* 7.52). Action in the drama can only be inferred from what we are told in the text. In *Prometheus Bound*, as we shall discover, there are a number of spectacular stage-effects which we can infer from the text. Note that exits and entrances take place by means of either the side-entrances between the *theatron* and the *skene* (see Figure 3) or through the stage door. In *Prometheus Bound*, all entrances and exits are by these side-entrances (*eisodoi* or *parodoi*).

b) Scenery

Aristotle (*Poetics*, 1449a) tells us that Sophocles introduced scene-painting, but it seems likely that, already in Aeschylus, the front of the *skene* was used to indicate the type of surrounding (for example, a palace front or, as in *Prometheus Bound*, a rocky landscape). We know nothing directly about this scenery, but we might reasonably conjecture that its scale and complexity were limited by the fact that, except for the first play of the day, each play had to follow on from the last, which may have required quite different scenery.

c) Masks

In all drama during our period, actors and chorus all acted in masks (which, as far as we can tell, were lifelike and covered the head; see *WA* 7.51 and illustration 7:10). The reasons for this are obscure and probably lie in the religious or ritual origins of Greek tragedy. However, apart from the practical consequence of allowing two or three actors to play a number of roles as clearly indicated by the restriction in number of actors, the result precluded a focus on the features of an individual actor interpreting a particular role – an aspect of theatrical drama that we now take more or less for granted, especially on TV. Note, however, that from at least the 440s there was a meeting a few days before the festival in Pericles' Odeion (built *c.*444 BCE – see Figure 1) where a preview was given of tragedies to be performed in the theatre, by actors without masks (to help audiences identify individual actors?). We have this information from a scholiast (later marginal commentator) on a passage from a fourth-century orator Aeschines, and also from Plato, *Symposium*, 194ff.

The mention of masks leads me to a final general point which I would like you to keep in mind while reading the four tragedies in this block. Greek drama was the reverse of intimate theatre: masks, stylized costume, formal diction and, above all, the enormous size of the Greek theatre (*c.*30 or 40 ft from *skene* to nearest audience and several hundred to the back of the theatre (see Figure 3) – all lead us to assume a 'large' rhetorical delivery of speech accompanied by ample gesture (a quality of presentation which the actors have tried to convey verbally in the Performance Cassettes). Subtle visual detail, of the kind favoured by the 'close-up' of TV production, would not have been part of the technique. Please try to keep in mind what you have learned in this section about the visual aspect of Greek tragedy while you read the four plays in the block.

N.B. In this section I have occasionally referred to TVs 1–3. Please note that these three TV programmes have been made because drama is a visual as well as a verbal medium. TV is uniquely able to convey the visual aspects of drama beyond the capacity of the printed page. Viewing them is therefore an essential part of the work on this block.

2 *PROMETHEUS BOUND*

2.1 The *Prometheia* trilogy

In Section 1.3 above I noted that in the festival each tragedian was required to produce four plays (three tragedies and a lighter 'satyr' play). The three tragedies were either closely related as one story in separate parts (a trilogy), or were three plays more loosely connected. Most of our surviving Greek tragedies belong to sets of the latter kind, and we have only one full trilogy, the *Oresteia* of Aeschylus. *Prometheus Bound* is probably the surviving play of another trilogy where we have only fragments of the other plays. When studying *Prometheus Bound* in detail, we shall try to place it in its context in the trilogy, as far as we can reconstruct it.

You may have been somewhat surprised to read, in *WA* 7.36 (final paragraph), that Prometheus is 'probably not by [Aeschylus]'. The question of authenticity is a fairly recent and unresolved controversy. There was no doubt in the ancient world about Aeschylus' authorship, but firm external evidence – such as we have for many other plays, as well as author, date and circumstances of production, details which date from the Alexandrian commentators' systematic cataloguing of the plays in the third century BCE – is not available for

Prometheus Bound. In addition, scholars have analysed what they judge to be 'un-Aeschylean' features of language, metre, style and themes (based, admittedly, on only six other plays!). To explain fully the controversy would take up most of this block, and it is not strictly necessary for our purposes to engage in it. Most scholars would agree that, if the play is not by Aeschylus, it was composed after his death, between the 450s and 430s BCE. We are not one hundred per cent certain that *Prometheus Bound* belonged to a trilogy, including the plays *Prometheus the Fire-bearer* and *Prometheus Unbound*, or if it did, whether it was the first or second play.

You may find this degree of uncertainty surrounding one of the four main texts for this block initially somewhat disconcerting. My advice is not to let this worry you; as you have already seen (in Block 1, Section 1), the problem of survival of evidence in the study of the fifth century BCE in Greece makes working with a greater or lesser degree of uncertainty inevitable. I intend here to take the advice of an editor of the play, Mark Griffith: 'Our first duty is to understand [*Prometheus Bound*] itself, on its own terms' (Aeschylus, *Prometheus Bound*, ed. M.Griffith, Cambridge University Press, 1983, p.35). For a brief review of the controversy, see Griffith, pp.30–35. To avoid continual circumlocution and explanation, the author of *Prometheus Bound* will henceforth be referred to as 'Aeschylus', but please bear in mind the reservation expressed above.

2.2 Prometheus in Greek myth

I stated above (end of 1.4) that the subject-matter of Greek tragedies was myth and legend, but that these were subject to interpretation in their dramatic realization by individual tragedians. We can now consider what this means in a specific case.

The original audience in the theatre would, as part of their heritage, already know the basic story, much as the audience at a medieval mystery play would have known the biblical background. In order to put ourselves in the same position, or as near it as we can, we need to find out what the Athenian audience would have known about the subject of the play before coming to the theatre.

Most of our evidence (and, of course, the Athenians would probably have had more) comes from the seventh-century BCE poet Hesiod, whose poem *Theogony* (literally 'birth' or 'genealogy of the gods'), along with the stories of Homer, gave the Greeks much of their belief about the remote past. (For Homer and Hesiod, see *WA Glossary*.)

Let us now look at what we know about Prometheus. In asking you to read the following stories, my purpose is not merely to look at 'origins' for the sake of it; but in seeing what the playwright chooses to make of the traditions, we can gain a major insight into his conception and purpose.

Please read WA 2.9 (from the bottom of p.93 to the top of p.96). While reading these two passages of Hesiod, please make a note of the main points of the stories and consider what we learn about (a) Prometheus' position with regard to Gods and mortals; (b) Hesiod's attitude to Prometheus.

Please carry on and read WA 2.10 on the general cultural significance of the stories.

Discussion _____

First the main points:

1   The stories from Hesiod related at *WA* 2.9 tell us about Prometheus, a wily trickster: whatever its origins, his name was taken by the Greeks to mean 'Forethought'. Along with other gods (his brothers) he is punished for insolence by Zeus, the king of the gods. Characteristically in this type of poetic composition, we hear of Prometheus' punishment before his crime, which was to deceive Zeus in setting out meat offerings in sacrifice by giving the

god the disguised inferior portion, an explanation of the Greek sacrificial practice of offering the bones to the gods (as Hesiod notes: *WA* p.94, end of first paragraph). In addition, when Zeus in revenge deprived mortals of the use of fire, Prometheus stole it back for them. In punishment he was bound to a pillar and preyed on by an eagle until finally rescued by the demi-god Herakles.

2   In the other story – the creation of the woman Pandora – Prometheus plays a subsidiary role, warning his less intelligent brother Epimetheus ('Afterthought') not to receive Zeus' fatal gift. Note how the same story is given a slightly different treatment in each of the two versions.

On the questions:

a)   Prometheus clearly belongs to a family of minor deities whose power is limited. His main activity consists of attempting to gain advantage over Zeus by trickery. However, his tricks (the deception at the sacrifice and the theft of fire), for which he is severely punished, both associate him closely with humans and concern in particular the relationship between the gods (especially Zeus) and the human race, in which Prometheus appears to act as a kind of mediator. Note, however, the ambivalent effect of Prometheus' 'mediation'. His first trick at the sacrifice (in Hesiod we are given no other motive than 'great cunning') brings down the wrath of Zeus on mortals, which leads to Prometheus' more positive acts – the stealing of fire and advising against the acceptance of Pandora.

b)   For Hesiod, Prometheus is 'wily' (the epithet occurs several times in the passages, although he is 'brave' when he steals fire), and the main emphasis in the stories is on the highly undesirable consequences for mortals of getting on the wrong side of Zeus. Hesiod believes that the human race has, largely through its own wickedness, but aided by tricksters like Prometheus, declined from an original Golden Age in the past, when, as in the Mekone sacrifice, gods and men originally came together. Its present existence is one of unremitting toil and hardship. ♦

In fifth-century Athens, Prometheus was a minor deity (not one of the Olympian gods) particularly associated with craftsmen (for example, potters), and his cult was celebrated at the Athenian festival of the Prometheia. A fire-giver (very often a fire-stealer), whether divine, human or animal, is a central figure in the myths of a wide variety of civilizations, and fire's significance in connection with warmth, food and crafts is universal. Why Prometheus should be associated with mortals in this way in Greek mythology is unknown. But note, finally, that the tradition already contains the seeds of an ambivalent relationship – Prometheus as saving the human race or contributing to its downfall? Foresight or merely cunning? We shall see in a moment what Aeschylus makes of this.

2.3   The play

We shall now study *Prometheus Bound* in detail.

In a moment I would like you to read the whole play through quite quickly in order to gain an overall impression. The following points are intended to help you in this initial reading.

1   Note the overall structure of the play (discussed in general terms in 1.5 above). A prelude is followed by the entry of the Chorus (p.25). The remainder of the play alternates dialogue and chorus, until the Chorus exit, unconventionally, at the end (p.52).

2   Another way of looking at the structure is to focus on the central character, Prometheus. He is on stage and totally immobile throughout the play, until

plunged underground at the end by Zeus' thunderbolt. However, the play is structured clearly and symmetrically by means of his encounter with different characters: first Oceanus (god), pp.29–32; then Io (mortal), pp.37–46; and finally Hermes (god), pp.48–52. The play's impetus stems from Prometheus' relationships with these characters, and his developing perception of his own position in relationship to the absent but overseeing Zeus. Note in particular that a vital aspect of the original myth, the emphasis upon the relationship between Gods and mortals, is here given central importance through the person of Prometheus, the god who helps mortals in defiance of Zeus. Moreover, his encounter with Io (the only mortal character in the play) is not only the longest (more than 300 lines) but is pivotal in taking us from Prometheus' self-agonizing to his open defiance of Hermes (and so, Zeus) which leads to the violent ending of the play. While you read, try to remain aware of how this development in Prometheus takes place.

3   Note that the action of the play represents a very small part of the total 'myth of Prometheus', namely an early stage in his punishment. Yet the apparently restricted scope is belied by the characters who in their speeches broaden the theme to take in the whole myth, ranging from the battle of gods and Titans and the theft of fire, related by Prometheus himself (pp.27–8), to prediction and foreshadowing of the future, especially the fate of Prometheus and of Zeus. This latter should remind us of a point I made above (2.1) that this play may well be the first or second of a trilogy and that much of what takes place within it can be related to the other plays, and especially the final play, *Prometheus Unbound*, in which there is probably some kind of reconciliation or 'deal' between Prometheus and Zeus.

4   You may not find the play easy reading at first; in preparing this block, it struck me that the long and involved geographical detail of the narrative of Io's wanderings (lines 640–875) represents perhaps the most difficult hurdle for those attempting a first encounter with Greek tragedy. But when reading this section, try to bear in mind:

a)   The attraction for its own sake of geographical description of an exotic 'far-away' type for the playwright's audience. The fifth century saw an expansion of knowledge of, and interest in, peoples and places far removed geographically and culturally from the Greek *polis*, as the writings of Herodotus testify, for example. A theatre audience would nevertheless have accepted the (to us) geographical/mythical mishmash and would not have been critical of his numerous inaccuracies. (For help with this section, please consult the map, Figure 5.)

b)   Io's 'story' is organically connected to the plot as she is the ancestor of Herakles, who was destined to become Prometheus' liberator (a Greek audience would have swiftly picked this up). Moreover, her fate at the hands of Zeus (lines 649–83) also illustrates further the central theme of human suffering at the hands of the gods.

5   Finally, as you read through, try to be alert to the vocabulary used, especially words and phrases with political significance, such as 'tyranny' and 'justice', and words concerned with 'wisdom' and 'prudence'. We shall, as far as we can in a translation, be looking at the language of the play, and how it contributes to thematic development.

Now please read the play through. While doing so, try to envisage a theatre performance, using information already given in 1.5 above, and the translator's stage directions. While reading, or independently of reading if you wish, you should also listen to the performance of Prometheus Bound *on Cassette 6, Band 2.*

PERFORMANCE

16

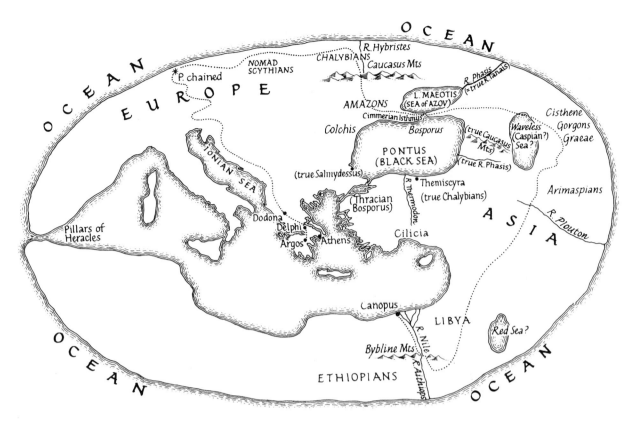

Figure 5 A modern hypothetical reconstruction of the wanderings of Io, based on *Prometheus Bound*, lines 700–875 (from Aeschylus, *Prometheus Bound*, ed. M. Griffith, Cambridge, Cambridge University Press, 1983, p.vi).

Using the Performance Cassette

From time to time, student exercises will assume that you have listened to the Performance Cassette: it is essential to listen as well as read if you are going to get the full benefit from the play as performance. You should also assume from now on that instructions to re-read a given section of the play imply also that you should replay the relevant section on the cassette. You may find it useful to locate sections quickly by noting the number on your cassette player's digital counter at key points in the performance, and writing it into your text of the play, for example, the entry of the Chorus, of Oceanus, of Io and of Hermes.

Noting your place on the Performance Cassette is important because from time to time you will need to replace it with the Interactive Cassette, Cassette 1, which you will need in several of the sections which follow.

(These instructions will also apply to the playing of Performance Cassette 7, which will accompany your reading of Sophocles' *Antigone* in Section 4 of this block.)

Note that, on the Performance Cassettes as a whole, the Chorus is one voice only (we experimented unsuccessfully with other techniques). In the original, much of the Chorus part of the play (we don't know exactly how much) would have been *sung* by multiple voices.

From this point I shall assume that you have read the play through; I shall now take it section by section.

N.B. In order to find individual line numbers, locate the numbers given at the top of each page and then count down or up. As the numbering in your translation is not always consistent, especially in the choral odes, the line numbers indicated here may not always coincide with your counting. It is usually obvious which passages are being referred to.

2.4 Prometheus, Hephaestus and Oceanus: Gods and gods

The first section of the play, in which the playwright concentrates chiefly on Prometheus' 'crime' and its punishment, itself can be divided into three sub-sections, delineated by the entrance and/or exit of characters.

1 Prometheus being bound to the rock by Hephaestus, overseen by Strength (lines 1–84).

2 Prometheus' soliloquy and the arrival of the Chorus, daughters of Oceanus (85–283).

3 The entry of Oceanus and his dialogue with Prometheus, followed by his exit (284–396).

2.4.1 Lines 1–84

Note that your translation *may* have a misprint in the line numbers given at the top of pp.23–24; they should read 69–92 and 93–126 respectively.

Please re-read 1–84. As you do so, consider, and make notes in answer to, the following questions:

1 *In your opinion, what are the dramatic qualities of this opening scene?*

2 *What themes are introduced, and how?*

Discussion

There are a number of points here: at this stage you should not be discouraged if you failed to notice all of them.

1 *Dramatic impact*

a) The first point which strikes me is the setting, 'A rocky mountain top, within sight of the sea'. This scene – as the translator reasonably infers, from lines 5, 20 and 89 for example – may have required one or two props, such as the rock; but the details would mostly have been left to the audience's imagination. This would demand greater imagination, one supposes, than the more usual 'palace front' which many tragedies required (including, Sophocles' *Antigone*, which you will be reading after *Prometheus Bound*). We are overlooking Ocean, which was the end of the Greek world (see Figure 5). The atmosphere of remoteness is underlined by the opening words of the play. This background contributes to an arresting opening, with Prometheus dragged, we may infer, through one of the *eisodoi* (see Figures 3 and 4) and onto the stage.

b) Two speaking characters are involved in this scene in minor 'introductory' roles. By a common Greek perception, one of them, Strength, is seen as a personification of his function (the Greek word strongly indicates physical force). Hephaestus is a minor deity, in Athens associated in cult with Prometheus; as the God of Fire, he is also closely connected with Prometheus' 'crime'. There are also two silent characters: first Violence, a 'walk-on' part, but also, much more important, Prometheus himself, whose silence until line 85 is dramatically significant.

c) There is a formally arranged dialogue: each character has an opening speech (1–35) followed by a swift exchange of lines (36–78), followed by Strength's final speech to Prometheus (79–84). This swift exchange (known in Greek as *stichomythia*: Figure 4) is accompanied by violent action, the binding of Prometheus. Note that tension is sustained by the way in which the words of one speaker are picked up and used to advantage against him by the other (see especially 45–6 *hate*; 66–8 *weep/weeping/pity*; 69–70 *see/ see*). There is lively interaction between them, Strength's two lines to Hephaestus' one indicating Strength's predominance. You should note particularly the dynamic effect of this exchange on the Performance Cassette.

The use of *stichomythia* to represent a kind of verbal duel (though on this occasion a very one-sided fight) will feature prominently in other drama in the course.

2   Themes

You may recall what was said above (2.2) concerning the audience's advance knowledge of the myth, though note that the identity of the characters is swiftly established. What the author is concerned with here is establishing which aspect(s) of the myth he will emphasize and which themes he will use. In this connection, I would note the following:

a)   The emphasis on the inexorable power of Zeus (the Greek implies 'tyranny' rather than 'sovereignty' in line 10), seen through the brutality (for example, 57ff.) and cynicism (for example, 79 ff.) of his henchman, Strength, who executes orders without compassion and advises Hephaestus to do the same. For Strength, Prometheus is a villain (a better translation than 'rebel' in line 4) and a fool; note the ironic use of Prometheus' name in 82. His master, Zeus, although absent, sees everything and hears everything. The 'presence' of the 'absent' Zeus is of major dramatic importance throughout the play. Note also that Zeus' power derives its harshness from recent acquisition: 'Power newly won is always harsh' (35).

b)   Hephaestus is forced to bind Prometheus (his 'duty' [line 3] as the god associated with metal-working), and his compassion for the pain and suffering caused is nevertheless accompanied by a belief that Zeus' authority must be acknowledged and obeyed. Prometheus was 'transgressing right' in helping mortals (30).

c)   In this opening section, the playwright is also introducing certain oppositions or tensions between ideas:

   •   Violence (physical cruelty, indifference to suffering) opposed to pity and fellow-feeling (for example, Hephaestus' concern for Prometheus, Prometheus' championing of the human race).

   •   Wisdom/folly. I noted above Strength's ironic use of Prometheus' name in 82. 'You're wrongly named Prometheus, Wise-before-the-event!/Wisdom is just the thing you want'. This opening section of the play introduces the initial Zeus-inspired perception of Prometheus' proverbial 'wisdom'; see especially 10, where Prometheus needs to be 'taught' acceptance; 62, where he needs to learn, translating literally, 'that he is a *sophistes* more stupid than Zeus' (*sophistes* = 'wise man', but with a probable pejorative connotation; you will learn about 'sophists' in Block 5). The irony and paradox of the 'forethinker' as a fool needing to be taught foreshadows the importance of this theme in the play as a whole.   ◆

One final question: in the polarity between violence and compassion, on which side would you place 'Right' (or 'Justice')?

Discussion

I hope you resisted the temptation to place it automatically with compassion and pity. Please note that at this stage the only reference to Right (the Greek is better translated as 'Justice') by Hephaestus (who is, after all, sympathetic to Prometheus) in 30, suggests that what Prometheus did in stealing fire, was 'transgressing right'.   ◆

The scene taken as a whole

Besides being a dramatically arresting introduction, the opening scene sets out the main conflict of the play by means of a series of oppositions:

- Zeus, through his henchman Strength, to Prometheus;

- Gods to mortals (though Prometheus is divine, he has chosen suffering on behalf of humans);

- (Effective) violence to (ineffective) compassion.

Hephaestus does not appear again – all characters in this play appear only once – but his sympathetic acquiescence serves to mark out more strongly Prometheus' refusal to accept Zeus as master. And all this before the central character has even opened his mouth!

In looking back on this scene, note how my distinction between dramatic and thematic aspects seems, in retrospect, rather artificial. The visual aspect of Prometheus' punishment is closely connected with the theme of brutal violence; and – through the lively dialogue, which was surely aimed to gain the audience's initial attention – the audience is also engaged at an intellectual level with the main themes of the play.

2.4.2 Lines 85–284

At this point, please select the first Interactive Cassette, Cassette 1, and wind it to Band 2. Have your Television and Audio-cassette Notes to hand.

INTERACTIVE

1

1 *Prometheus speaking alone (85–127)* SECTION ONE (88-128)

The discussion of this scene will be entirely on cassette. Before you begin, please read the introductory note to Band 2 in the Television and Audio-cassette Notes. Then switch on.

You should not proceed until you have finished the first section of Band 2 of Cassette 1.

2 *Prometheus and the Chorus (128–284)*

We come now to a major dramatic point in the play, the entry of the Chorus (*parodos*). The Chorus are daughters of Ocean, the sea which the Greeks believed surrounded the earth and which Prometheus' crag overlooks (see Figure 5). Their entrance was probably spectacular, if to us, perhaps, a trifle bizarre: they have flown in a winged carriage (136). How was this brought on stage? Swung through the air by means of a crane (with many Chorus men on board!)? Pushed on stage? Or did each Chorus member have (his) own? Or (as has been suggested) are the conveyances supposed to be imagined as present? Or are they imagined as 'parked' off-stage? We just don't know. We can, however, assume that the effect was visually arresting: note that we are given plenty of time for the Chorus to traverse the considerable distance to the orchestra from the *parodoi* (Figure 3). A very common feature of entrances is their 'signalling' by characters already on stage. Prometheus cannot move, and so see them entering, but he can hear them, and his fear is a dramatically effective way of registering their approach (113–27).

Please now re-read 128–92. While doing so, consider what role or roles the Chorus play in their first exchanges with Prometheus.

Discussion _____

a) The first point I would make concerns the visual impact. Recall the point I made in Section 1.5 concerning the visual prominence of the Chorus. Their entrance would have been eye-catching, and they are initially involved in a lyric exchange with Prometheus. While they sing they would possibly also have performed a dance in the *orchestra*, addressing the immobile Prometheus on stage.

b) The Chorus form a sympathetic audience for Prometheus. Like Hephaestus (and later their father Oceanus), they are part of the less powerful group of minor deities who disapprove of what Zeus has done, but are not able or willing to oppose him. They are brave even to come: 'quiet bashfulness' (134) translates Greek *aidos*, an emotion which Athenian men thought appropriate for women.

c) Their sympathy is mixed with disapproval of Prometheus' 'freedom of speech' (178): he is too defiant.

In the course of Prometheus' first scene with the Chorus (which in 193 settles into dialogue metre), two more themes begin to come into prominence alongside the continually repeated theme of arbitrary violence and extreme suffering:

1 Hints are given that Zeus may be overthrown by a plot (165–6) and that all-knowing Prometheus may have the secret which he can trade for his freedom (167–75).

2 The perspective is extended backwards to Prometheus' offence and the war among the gods which preceded it (199ff.). ◆

Please now read lines 199–256 which tell the basic myth. At the same time you need to compare this with the Hesiod passages introduced in Section 2.2 above, and also look at ST 14(a) (an extract from the battle of Zeus and the Titans in Hesiod's Theogony). There are fundamental differences between the myth of the battle of the gods and the theft of fire in Hesiod and this play.

a) Can you list them?

b) What do they tell us about Aeschylus' perception and treatment of the story?

Discussion _____

a) The mythical elements

   i) The battle of Zeus and the Titans

- In this play, as opposed to Hesiod, Zeus' victory has no air of finality about it. What Prometheus knows is still dangerous to Zeus.

- In the play, Prometheus is a key figure in the overthrow, whereas he doesn't figure at all in Hesiod. In Hesiod, Zeus wins by force, in the play by cunning, aided by Prometheus' intelligence. In the play, Prometheus is prominent in advising, first the Titans and then, when they ignore him, Zeus himself.

- Prometheus' increased importance is indicated by making him a son of Themis (or Earth) who possesses the secret of Zeus' downfall. In Hesiod, Prometheus is a son of Clymene, a daughter of Oceanus, of very minor importance.

   ii) The theft of fire

In the play, Prometheus' theft of fire is simply an attempt to save the human race, in reaction to Zeus' decision to annihilate it (we don't know from the play why Zeus made this initial decision). But in Hesiod, the theft answers Zeus' retaliation for Prometheus' other deception of Zeus at the Mekone sacrifice, which *Prometheus Bound* does not mention (nor does this play refer to Pandora).

b) Aeschylus' perception of the myth

It is quite possible that the differences from Hesiod are Aeschylus' invention – though, as so often in Greek culture, we cannot prove the negative, because no other literary treatments of the Prometheus legend survive. It is one of the

Figure 6 Attic red-figure calyx-krater by the Dinos painter (425–420). The lower scene shows satyrs lighting their torches from the fire stolen by Prometheus in a fennel stalk (after *Prometheus the Fire Raiser*, a satyr play produced in 472 BCE, in a tetralogy which included *The Persians*). (Oxford, Ashmolean Museum; 1937.983, ARV1153 no.13.)

remarkable characteristics of the Greeks' perception of their own mythical tradition that radical innovations by individuals were perfectly acceptable (contrast the probable reaction of a modern Christian audience to a *major* change in details or emphasis in the Gospel story). If, then, Aeschylus was largely responsible for the prominent position of Prometheus in the play, and his opposition to Zeus on behalf of the human race, this must be because the playwright wished to emphasize the conflict of Zeus and Prometheus rather than simply, as in Hesiod, offer a mythical explanation of the present situation, i.e. the presence of toil and trouble in human life. Moreover, the absence of reference, in this play at least, to the Mekone sacrifice, makes Zeus' motivation in moving against the human race appear more arbitrary and Prometheus' action in defending the human race more obviously *philanthropia* (literally, 'love of the human race') as his enemies assert (for example, Strength at 11). Mark Griffith (op. cit., p.5) remarks on the 'transformation of Hesiod's morality tale into a drama of tragic tone and proportions'.

Yet note also the clear evidence in 199ff. that Prometheus was no knight in shining armour. When the Titans refused his advice, Prometheus changed his allegiance to Zeus, and his help (we don't know what it was) turned out to be decisive. His explanation in 216–17 is expressed in terms of political pragmatism ('it seemed best ' implies, in Greek, 'most advantageous'). The 'tyrant's disease' Prometheus complains about in 224–5 refers to Zeus' inability to trust his 'friends' (*philoi*: the Greek has a strong overtone of 'political ally').

Can we (should we) reconcile the political pragmatist and the philanthropic saviour of the human race (234–6)? This question will be picked up in Section 2.7, and in Section 6. ♦

2.4.3 Lines 285–396 (Prometheus and Oceanus)

Read this episode now, considering:

a) *what you think of its dramatic qualities;*
b) *the nature of the relationship between Prometheus and Oceanus.*

(In considering how you would answer these questions, be sure to listen to the scene as played on the Performance Cassette: Cassette 6, Band 2.)

Discussion

a) The first impression you may gain is that the episode is not dramatically very effective. Oceanus' arrival is spectacular: he is seated on a winged creature and may have been swung down into the theatre on a crane. But he comes unannounced and out of the blue, and interrupts Prometheus' intention to reveal the future to the Chorus (272ff.). Griffith (op. cit.) regards this interruption, seen as a device for maintaining suspense, as 'rather crude, but effective' (note on 283ff.). But note that the Chorus is totally ignored by Oceanus (their father!). Some editors have assumed either that they move out of sight behind the *skene* at this point (difficult to relate to the text) or, more plausibly, that in their initial conversation with Prometheus (128ff.) they do not descend into the *orchestra*, but stay perhaps on the roof of the *skene*, descending to ground level during the Prometheus/ Oceanus scene, and so, with greater dramatic plausibility, take no further part in the dialogue. Griffith has a full discussion of this whole question (see Griffith, op. cit., note on 128–9).

b) Oceanus is a 'friendly warner', a not uncommon figure in tragic drama, giving advice which, when rejected by the central character, may serve to heighten the dramatic tension, the heroic individuality of the recipient and the tragic outcome. Oceanus' dialogue with Prometheus serves to give greater point to the suggestion – already made by Hephaestus (28ff.) and the Chorus (259ff.) – that Prometheus should give in and change his attitude towards Zeus. I hope you noted especially:

  i) The closely argued exchange at 376–92, in which each speaker takes up, and turns to advantage, the remarks of the other (see the discussion in Section 2.4.1, of the more one-sided dialogue between Strength and Hephaestus). This type of 'diamond-cut-diamond' exchange was keenly appreciated by Athenians in a variety of contexts (especially legal and philosophical, as you will discover in Block 5).

  ii) The shift in relationships during the scene. Prometheus is initially friendly, but by 392 he has lost his temper. Conversely, Oceanus starts by professing constancy and willingness to help (295–7), but Prometheus' attitude leads him to abandon his task and hastily head for home (394–6). Note the way, in 384–7, that 'wisdom' and 'folly' are incorporated into the paradoxical exchanges between the two speakers.

  iii) Note the digression on the fate of two opponents of Zeus (347–73). As we shall see in the next section, a feature of the play is extended mythical and geographical reference. There is also a note (347ff.) on the origin of volcanic activity and a possible reference (366–73) to an actual eruption of Etna in 479 or 475 BCE. But these 'digressions' turn out to be very much to the point: they demonstrate Prometheus' courage (he can expect at least as grim a fate) and compassion for his fellow Titans. These two qualities, especially the latter, become important in the next section. ◆

On reading through this section in draft, I felt dissatisfied with my analysis in (ii) above. Do you think that in (ii) I have dealt adequately with this scene? (Think particularly of the scene as played on the Performance Cassette.)

Discussion _____

The analysis of the structure is adequate as far as it goes, but I have to confess that I find it quite difficult to judge the *tone* of the exchange. Is Prometheus being sarcastic in 331–5, and especially 341ff? What sort of character is Oceanus? A sincere helper or a pompous humbug? You may be interested to note that these uncertainties were felt by the actors playing Prometheus and Oceanus on the Performance Cassette. Do you think they got it right? (Play it again if you can't remember.) Even trying to answer this question will take you into the problem of whether we can speak of 'character' in the modern sense – and this I wish to leave for the moment. You will return to it in Section 4.5.2. ◆

2.5 Prometheus and Io: Gods and mortals

In this long middle section of the play (lines 397–884), one of the themes of the Prometheus story – the relationship of Gods and mortals – comes into the foreground. The four sections into which it can be divided show an increasingly explicit reference to the human race and its relationship with Zeus: firstly, in the Chorus (397–437), which tells of the grief of the peoples of the world at the fate of Prometheus and his brothers; secondly, in the account by Prometheus of the consequences for human development of his gift of fire (438–525); thirdly, another passage in which the Chorus assert the need to bow to the will of Zeus (526–60); finally, most vividly and at greatest length, the episode with Io, the human victim of Zeus (561–884).

I shall now deal with each of these sections in turn.

Please re-read each one before turning to my commentary.

2.5.1 Lines 397–437 (Chorus) — *Choral Song*

This scene is the first *stasimon* of the Chorus.

For discussion of this scene, please listen to the second section of Cassette 1, Band 2. (To do this you will need to remove the Performance Cassette temporarily.) Switch on now.

INTERACTIVE

You should not continue until you have finished the second section of Band 2 of Cassette 1.

2.5.2 Lines 438–525 (Prometheus' exposition to the Chorus)

Prometheus (ignoring his interrupted promise to reveal the future in 272) now instructs the Chorus in how he taught mortals skills which transformed mortal life. Chief among these was the ability to reason, to acquire skills and hence develop the basics of civilization through the mastery of practical arts – use of animals in agriculture, the building of ships, discovery of minerals – and other skills with practical application, including knowledge of stars and seasons, number, writing and prophecy.

At this point, as well as re-reading the passage, please also read Hesiod's account of the development of the human race (ST 14(b)) and re-read the consequences of the theft of fire (WA, p.95). When you have done that, please consider two questions:

1   *What differences do you detect between Hesiod's conception of the history of the human race and that of Aeschylus?*

2   *Why should Aeschylus emphasize prophecy at such length (484–98)?*

1 Differences between Hesiod and Aeschylus

There is, I think, an immediate and overwhelming difference. Hesiod sees human history in pessimistic and regressive terms: Prometheus is responsible for human ills by provoking Zeus to withhold a livelihood from men and, moreover, inflicting women on them, at best a doubtful asset and at worst a liability. In his attitude to the role of women, Hesiod is here revealing an early *polis* peasant-farmer outlook. However, in the passage (*ST* 14(b)) which immediately follows the end of the *Works and Days* passage, quoted in *WA* (p.96), Hesiod outlines a comprehensive theory of human decline from an original Age of Gold, when humans lived like gods without worry, toil or the miseries of old age, in a world where all things were effortlessly available and they themselves were 'dear to the blessed gods' (*Works and Days*, 120). Our present generation, says Hesiod, is a race of iron, where 'there is no rest from labour by day nor from wasting away by night' (ibid., 176–8). And, Hesiod assures us, there is worse to come!

For Aeschylus on the other hand, the perspective is essentially progressive and optimistic: the human race, under the benevolent tutelage of Prometheus, has advanced from mindless misery to civilization (by implication, beneficial), through the acquisition of skills. The 'golden age' is not in the past, as in Hesiod, and may, by implication, be in the future.

These two opposed perspectives of human history had wide currency in the Classical world (see, for example, *ST* 9). In emphasizing very strongly the progressive perspective, and linking Prometheus with it, the playwright (from the point of view of this play at least) appears to be reflecting a confidence in human endeavour which takes place not only without Zeus' consent, but against his will. Ignorance of the content of the remainder of the trilogy makes it difficult to assess the total impact of this idea; however, in this play at least, a conflict between the outlook of mortals and that of Zeus seems to be proposed. Yet Aeschylus injects a note of sad irony which is absent in Hesiod: for all his activity on behalf of mortals, the one person Prometheus is unable to help, it appears, is himself. He is 'like a bad doctor fallen ill' (475) – a metaphor of disease and cure, in the light of which Prometheus' assertion of his own success in this area on behalf of mortals has an ironic undertone (478–83).

2 The emphasis upon prophecy and divination (484–98)

Why does Aeschylus single out this subject? Though it's not immediately obvious, I suggest that learning about this subject is related to the theme of the relationship between gods and mortals since divination is part of learning the will of the gods. According to Hesiod, it was at a sacrifice – a crucial element in the mortal/god relationship – that, through Prometheus, gods and humans became estranged. Here in the play, Prometheus is perhaps showing how he led mortals back to a satisfactory relationship with the gods. But there is a tension between Prometheus' ability to teach the 'various modes of prophecy' (484) to mortals, his own attitude to learning, often seen through the eyes of others in the play, and his own relationship to the (other) gods.

At the end of this section, we see a foreshadowing of the future (see also 167–75): the audience is being led increasingly to consider the possibility that Prometheus may be freed and Zeus' attitude may change. We recall Hesiod's bald statement concerning the freeing of Prometheus, to which Zeus did not object: 'And he ceased from the rage he had felt against Prometheus for his defiance of the will of almighty Zeus' (*WA*, p.94). In the play at this point, however, we are still envisaging the possibility that Zeus may be overthrown (see Chorus at 505). ◆

The idea of human progress (443–502) will be discussed further in a broader context in Section 6.1 below.

2.5.3 Lines 526–60 (Chorus)

In their second *stasimon*, the Chorus assert the need to treat the gods with due reverence. Their concern for Prometheus does not extend to approval of his actions: 'You respect too highly the race of mortals' (542). Zeus' government is described as a 'harmony' (551: the Greek *harmonia* implies 'established order' without necessarily an overtone of moral approval). Humans (remember, the speakers are deities) are creatures who 'live for a day' (548) who cannot give Prometheus any help now that he needs it.

This pessimistic view of the potential of humans put forward by the Chorus contrasts with the optimistic view of Prometheus in the previous passage.

Can you account for this contrast in views?

Discussion _____

The Chorus do not share Prometheus' feelings about the human race; their more conventional sentiments serve to emphasize Prometheus' isolation and bravery. Although much more sympathetic, they share the view of Prometheus' enemies, that he is 'foolhardy'. This idea will be taken up in greater depth in 2.7.2 below. ♦

2.5.4 Lines 561–884 (Prometheus and Io)

You may find it useful to read the following paragraph before you re-read this section of the play.

This section is the longest (almost one-third of the play) and in many respects the most difficult, dramatically and thematically, of the whole work. Before we embark on it, here are two initial points which may help you to clarify your reading. Io's basic functions in the play are two (related):

a) Like Prometheus, she is a victim of the ruthless power of Zeus, this time in the form of his sexual desire.

b) Her wanderings take up what seems to be a bewildering amount of space in this section of the play. Yet the point of Prometheus' long narration is clear at its end, when he foretells that in Egypt Io finally will bear to Zeus the ancestor of Herakles, Prometheus' liberator. An obscure mythological connection? We may think so, but it would be unwise to assume that the original audience (for whom these myths were not academic but part of a living culture) felt the same.

At this point you should re-read 561–884, if you have not already done so.

In a play of spectacular effects, we can imagine Io's entrance as bizarre and arresting. Without preparation, the audience sees her spinning across the orchestra (and/or stage), shrieking from the sting of the gadfly, with cow-horns attached to her mask. Dramatically she represents the total antithesis of the completely immobile Prometheus.

Would the audience have known who she was? Initially, I think not. The connection with Prometheus was not, as far as we know, traditional. Indeed it may have been invented by Aeschylus. However, her initial speech drops a number of hints: by the time we reach the climax of her name (588), all the audience must have guessed it (and they are given more information by Prometheus at 589–91). Io's entry, however, is fortuitous (this happens rarely in tragedy); her wanderings have brought her to this deserted spot, and she does not know Prometheus' identity until he tells her at 610. The common denominator of their suffering is clearly established, however; they are both victims of Zeus' arbitrary power.

The structure of 607–885 is organized around four long narratives:

1 Io's story of her attempted seduction by Zeus (645–86).

26

2 Prometheus' first narrative: where Io must wander immediately after this (700–40).

3 Prometheus' second narrative: Io's further travels (787–818).

4 Prometheus' third narrative: Io's ultimate deliverance (825–68).

In order to understand how this works dramatically, I suggest that you consider first what comes between these narratives: look for a moment (before reading the narratives) at 607–42, 687–99, 741–86 and 819–22. What, dramatically, do we learn from these interludes?

Discussion

1 Aeschylus seems, through the action, to be making an explicit (and dramatically rather clumsy?) choice between his various themes. Note 631–4, where the Chorus retard the story simply by stopping Prometheus from going ahead with an account of Io's fate and ask her to tell them her story first. (You may remember that Oceanus equally abruptly interrupted Prometheus in recounting his trials (285).) At 778–87, Prometheus offers Io a choice between two prophesies – hearing about the remainder of her journey or about his deliverer (in fact he grants both). Nevertheless these retardations have two consequences:

   a) Sympathy is established between deities (albeit minor ones) and a mortal, based upon common descent. The Greek idea of the separateness of divine and human worlds – based upon the obvious differences that gods were immortal, lived in separate places, and had far greater power – was modified by the very common 'mixed births' (the offspring of gods and mortals) which occur in Greek mythology.

   b) We (the audience) are given the whole story of Io, and are kept in suspense as to its outcome and ultimate relevance.

2 Io's desire to commit suicide, as a way out of her sufferings, is ironically contrasted with Prometheus who, as a god, cannot die (752ff. and see 2.7.2 below). This leads naturally on to the much postponed theme of Prometheus' deliverance, until we suddenly see that Prometheus and Io have in common more than Zeus as their tormentor: *Io's descendant will free Prometheus* (772). At this moment the whole point of the episode becomes clear and we are given a glimpse of the far-distant future. ◆

Now to the narratives themselves: you will need to refer to the map of Io's wanderings (Figure 5) during this section.

The mating of Zeus with mortal women is a commonplace of Greek mythology, but note here (649–86) that it is seen not as a privilege for the woman concerned but as an aggressive move against an unwilling victim, in which the divine apparatus (including oracles) is ranged against Io: her account is calculated to win the audience's sympathy.

With regard to the other narratives, we shall not be exploring the mythological/geographical references in detail, but you should note the comments I made about geographical description in my points on the initial reading, Section 2.3 above. But the narratives are not there simply for their own intrinsic interest: at this point in the play we are made aware of the broadening of the playwright's canvas. Not only are Io's wanderings long and remote, but her ultimate destination in Egypt (845ff.) projects the action forward many generations into the future in the form of the story of the flight to Argos of the daughters of Danaus, descendants of Zeus and Io, which is the subject of Aeschylus' *The Suppliants* (pp.54–86 in the *Prometheus Bound* Penguin).

Now consider the Io scene as a whole. In what way do you consider that it changes the dramatic perspective of the play?

Discussion _____

I would like to suggest that in the Io scene Aeschylus has done two things:

a) He has put the action of the play, necessarily limited in time and space, into its vast, one might almost say cosmic, context. Even through the continual torture of Io, the ultimate salvation of Prometheus is clearly foreshadowed; indeed 869–73 represents his most explicit statement yet about the future.

b) At the same time, the widening of the perspective in no way mitigates the suffering of Io or the cruelty of Zeus. Io's exit (876–84) is as violent as her entrance. There is no hint of a possible reconciliation of the adversaries. The violence of Zeus, so far merely recounted or hinted at, comes to a physical climax in the next, and final, section of the play.   ◆

2.6   Prometheus and Hermes: Gods and gods (line 887–end)

PERFORMANCE

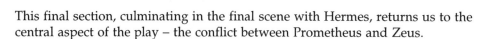

Re-read this section of the play now, with the Performance Cassette, Cassette 6. (Note that you will also need Cassette 1, Band 2 during this section.)

This final section, culminating in the final scene with Hermes, returns us to the central aspect of the play – the conflict between Prometheus and Zeus.

2.6.1   The Chorus (887–906)

Before we reach the final scene, read again what the Chorus say (887–906). With this in mind, briefly look back over the Chorus' role in the play so far, and ask the following questions:

a) *What are the Chorus singing about in 887–906, and how does this relate to the immediate context?*

b) *Starting out from your answer to (a), think about the role of the Chorus in the play generally. Do they represent any particular view, for example that of the audience or the playwright?*

Discussion _____

a) In 887–906 the Chorus are singing about the danger of a liaison with somebody of higher rank, or even a god. Yet the implication that there is choice in the matter stands in ironic juxtaposition to the Io scene, where Io clearly has had no choice whatever. And is there not a further irony in the 'dangerous marriage' theme if we look briefly at Prometheus' following speech, where it is Zeus' possible marriage (911), and not that of any mortal, which may well bring disaster upon *him*?

b) In 887–906 the ironies seem to be generated by the Chorus' ignorance of the implications of what they are saying. If we look at the part played by the Chorus earlier in the play, we can see that they have two main dramatic functions:

i) To react sympathetically, but not uncritically, to the plight and words of Prometheus (and Io). They strongly disapprove of the actions of the new gods (for example, 144ff.) but believe that resistance is useless and that Prometheus is too defiant and 'free with his words' (178ff.). They express the grief of the world at Prometheus' fate (397–435) but assert the need for feeble mortals to maintain good relations with the gods through worship (527–60). Prometheus was wrong to steal fire for mortals (260).

ii) To request and provide a receptive audience for the stories of Prometheus and Io (note how much of the play is taken up with the narration of stories).

TMA 02

28

The Chorus' role perhaps harmonizes with their character as 'modest' young girls only reluctantly permitted to come to Prometheus (130–4). Do their views represent those of Aeschylus? Our interpretation of 887–906 surely rules that out; unless this is completely mistaken, Aeschylus does not intend these Chorus sentiments to be taken at face value. And, by the same token, what the Chorus say puts them a long way behind the 'ideal spectator,' who, as I have suggested, is guided towards ironies unsuspected by the Chorus.

Yet the Chorus are not just 'another character': their role is different and performed in a different place (the *orchestra*) and in a different way; unlike the other characters, they take part in the play throughout. They contribute to the play by expressing a particular point of view which becomes generalized by conventional moralizing backed up by reference to other stories of myth. So the Chorus broadens the scope of the play on the moral issues involved (just as the Io episode broadens the historical and geographical framework). And, to look forward for a moment, note the unexpected ending: just as their compassion overcame their timidity at the time of their first appearance (128), so at the end they choose to stay with Prometheus after all, despite Hermes' threats (1061–7). This choice has marked dramatic significance, although it is uncertain what happens to the Chorus at the end of the play; 'Chorus scatter in all directions' is a reasonable translator's inference. ♦

After the Chorus, Prometheus continues his defiance of Zeus (910–42), predicting a future marriage which will destroy him. This leads directly to the following scene.

2.6.2 Prometheus and Hermes (943–end)

Structurally, this final scene relates closely to the opening scene of the play, in that the power of Zeus is brought again to the foreground through the entry of a messenger who is sent from him, leading to an altercation (cf. Strength and Hephaestus: 36–87). Hermes' entry is motivated by Prometheus' previous threatening speech; despite (because of?) the absence of Zeus, we are again made immediately aware of his all-seeing, all-hearing presence (see 53).

INTERACTIVE

At this point please listen to the Interactive Cassette, Cassette 1, Band 2, third section. You should not proceed until you have finished listening to this section of Cassette 1.

Now that you have read the passage and looked at verbal aspects of a section of it, what are the similarities and differences between this scene and the first of the play?

Discussion _____

a) First, the similarities. There is a similar emphasis upon Prometheus' cleverness as folly; for example, 'master-mind' in 944, like 'all his wisdom' in 62, translates the Greek *sophistes* = 'sophist'. He emphasizes his own defiance (960, cf. 29); his adversary recommends obedience as expedient (cf. Strength to Hephaestus 36ff.).

b) The differences are more obvious. The representative of Zeus is not a real minion, but one of the junior Olympians, Hermes, a god whose ambivalent nature as both messenger and god of trickery and deception (see *WA* Glossary) lends point to his role here. His presence makes it clear that a climax is approaching: Zeus is worried. Hermes' status also makes more daring Prometheus' insults ('his runner', 'lickspittle' – 941).

c) The other major difference is, of course, that Prometheus is no longer silent but violently and recklessly voluble. There is a tense argument in *stichomythia* similar to that between Strength/Hephaestus and Prometheus/Oceanus, with the same verbal 'capping' of argument; but this time the exchange is more acrimonious, as you saw from the Interactive Cassette. More is at stake. Prometheus' total lack of restraint (censured by both Hermes and the Chorus) leads directly to the final cataclysm. ♦

In this final scene, the main themes of the play – defiance of Zeus, Prometheus' suffering and foreknowledge of the future – all appear in extended form. At the insistence of Hermes, Prometheus (like the prophetess Cassandra in Aeschylus' *Agamemnon*) now reveals truth without 'clever riddles' (950), namely the downfall of Zeus (958). He also demonstrates his ability to see through long stretches of future time, which he asserts 'teaches everything' (981). Yet this, too, has its ironies. In the following line, Prometheus' inability to learn 'self-control' (*sophrosune*: see *WA* Glossary *sophron*) reminds us that in this play there are different conceptions of what constitutes 'wisdom'. On the one hand Prometheus' knowledge of the future gives him power over Zeus, while his ability to teach and give others knowledge and reason allows him to help the human race. On the other hand this knowledge makes him a fool in the eyes of his enemies (and even his friends) because it is accompanied by stubbornness or self-will (*authadia*, for example, 1033). Without prudence (*sophrosune*) and wise counsel (*euboulia*), according to his enemies, Prometheus' wisdom is folly.

This all goes to show that when you are dealing with words for moral values, their significance depends on who is defining the value: for Prometheus, *sophrosune* has all the negative connotations of 'keeping ... noses clean' (*WA* Glossary) whereas for Hermes, and to a lesser extent the Chorus, it has a more positive value.

As a final exercise in this section, consider the way the alternatives of stubbornness, wise counsel and wisdom are deployed, with special reference to 1033–9: 'Wise counsel ... enemy's hands.'

Discussion

These lines incorporate the views of all three speakers, Hermes, Chorus and Prometheus. For Hermes and the Chorus, wise counsel is to be opposed to the stubbornness which makes Prometheus' wisdom folly, and coming from a man reputedly wise, is shameful. Prometheus' answer (the final occasion on which these concepts occur in this play) rejects entirely the idea that what is happening to him is shameful, and reasserts his 'foreknowledge' (1038), i.e. his claim to real wisdom.

This is the climax of the 'battle of ideas,' after which no further persuasion is attempted. Prometheus remains convinced of the reality of his wisdom and his honour; Hermes gives up in the face of words which are like those of 'lunatics' (1055). ♦

I have analysed the scene in what may seem over-intellectualized terms in order to show how important ideas are in the central conflict of the play. Hermes and Prometheus, as we have seen, conduct a debate, stick by their own definitions and budge not an inch from their polarized positions.

So the argument inevitably breaks down and this is, in a sense, the end of the play. But we must not forget the Chorus. In moving out of character (of the 'quiet bashfulness' of young maidens (134)), they quit the sidelines and throw their lot in with Prometheus (1061–7). This sudden change of the Chorus – a move 'centre stage' as it were – is a masterly dramatic stroke carefully placed, I feel, near the end of the play. They effectively demonstrate that in extreme circumstances *loyalty* overrules prudence (*sophrosune*), thereby forcing Hermes to include them, as well as Prometheus, in his denunciation of 'folly' (1074). Their decision not only reverses their own stance throughout the play but cuts across the Prometheus/Hermes debate by appealing to values of a different and, in this context, more basic order.

The play ends with Zeus' punishment of Prometheus, plunging him underground in an earthquake. How this event was staged, what actually happened to Prometheus and whether the Chorus was intended to stay with him at the end is not known. Normal convention suggests that they leave the *orchestra* (though on this occasion it must have been an unconventional exit, as the

Figure 7 Apulian calyx-krater by the Branca painter (3rd quarter of fourth century BCE). The scene seems to represent *Prometheus Unbound*, with Prometheus, the central figure, tied at the wrists to a rock (the archway) flanked by his saviour Herakles (on left) and his mother Earth (on right) with other figures from the myth. (Antikenmuseum Berlin, Staatliche Museen Preussischer Kulturbesitz, 1969.9.)

translator indicates). Prometheus' final words, in which he calls on Earth to see his suffering (1090–3), are clearly not a resolution of conflict, but point the audience towards the sequel. In their emotional power they recall his first words of the play at 85ff.

2.7 Concluding essays

In these essays, there is an attempt to pull together ideas on two central themes which were continually in the background of the detailed discussion above. My conclusions, however, are designed to suggest further questions!

2.7.1 Prometheus and Zeus: authority and defiance

But, in truth, I was averse from a catastrophe so feeble as that of reconciling the Champion with the Oppressor of mankind. The moral interest of the fable, which is so powerfully sustained by the sufferings and endurance of Prometheus, would be annihilated if we could conceive of him as unsaying his high language and quailing before his successful and perfidious adversary.

(Shelley, Preface to *Prometheus Unbound*)

Shelley's conscious decision to depart from the Greek resolution of the Prometheus/Zeus conflict reflects, as it probably helped to shape, the Romantic Movement's conception of Prometheus – the political rebel and saviour of humanity confronting tyranny and injustice. Let's consider for a moment whether this conception reflects that of the original playwright.

In the larger context of the *Prometheia* trilogy, we know that the conflict is resolved in the (probably) final play, *Prometheus Unbound*, where Prometheus is released (as predicted in *Prometheus Bound*, 871) and relinquishes his feud with Zeus. We have no idea when or how the feud is ended. Caution is required, especially in view of a fragment from *Prometheus Unbound* (Griffith, op. cit., pp.296–7, fr. X) which has Prometheus addressing Herakles, after his release, as 'this most beloved son of a hateful father'. This tells us that Prometheus released is still not reconciled. There is also the question of how Zeus ultimately becomes reconciled to Prometheus. Does he change his nature and learn moderation? Or does he become reconciled without essentially changing – does he recognize the political reality and 'do a deal' with Prometheus? These two positions have had many adherents; but here we are not really in a position to make a judgement since we know so little about the other plays, and their relationship to *Prometheus Bound*.

If, however, we concentrate on *Prometheus Bound* as a separate dramatic entity, the initial question comparing Shelley and Aeschylus is still worth asking. In TV1, Tom Paulin's specially commissioned play *Seize the Fire* owes a great deal to Shelley. The visual setting and Paulin's language and imagery forcefully place Prometheus in a contemporary context which may call to mind a variety of twentieth-century situations involving tyranny and heroic resistance.

At this point, ask yourself the following question:

Taking Seize the Fire *as a basis, consider whether or not Aeschylus'* Prometheus Bound *intends us to see the relationship essentially in Shelley's terms, with approval of the brave rebel and disapproval of the cruel tyrant.*

(See the TV Notes for TV1, and listen to the discussions of TV1 on Cassette 6, Band 1, 'The making of Seize the Fire', *and Band 3, 'Seize the Fire* and Aeschylus' *Prometheus Bound'; also, look over any notes you may have made yourself.)*

PERFORMANCE

Discussion

This is a question to which I do not think that there is a 'yes or no' answer. Zeus' tyranny is described as cruel and arbitrary (it is superfluous to list occasions on which this is said) and its maintenance, just like its original acquisition, is characterized by violence. But there are also aspects which, to us, may not harmonize with that conception: for example, 30, where Hephaestus, sympathetic to Prometheus, describes his action in helping mortals as 'transgressing right' (literally 'beyond justice'). Remember also that Zeus' rule is described by the Chorus as a 'harmony' (553) (though remember my comment, in 2.5.3, that the word does not necessarily have the positive moral connotation of our 'harmony'). So, in some sense, this power may be related to what Athenians would have recognized as at least *a* (if not *their*) conception of justice and order. And note that not only Oceanus, but the Chorus, continually advise Prometheus to abandon his intransigent attitude.

In Tom Paulin's play we don't really feel that Prometheus as champion of the human race needs moral justification, although his attitude towards human beings does alter through the play (from arrogance to acceptance). But this is where we need to beware of importing modern attitudes into Aeschylus. The fact that the Greeks did not, on the whole, expect their gods to show pity or fellow-feeling makes Prometheus' attitude remarkable, in being prepared to sacrifice himself, a god, for the sake of lesser beings with whom he need not concern himself. He is a Greek god, not a freedom-fighter. And note his earlier political complicity with Zeus. What were Prometheus' motives for backing Zeus against the Titans (199–227)? We are not told ('it seemed best...', 216, implies expediency as I noted above, p.22). The essence of Prometheus' complaint here seems to be Zeus' failure to stand by his 'friends' (226–7). This point would surely have been appreciated by an audience, for whom to do good to *philoi* (friends) and evil to *ekhthroi* (enemies) would have been basic. Political pragmatism seems to have been a feature of the original alliance; and, as we might conjecture, may well have been a feature of the final reconciliation.

Moral disapproval of the gods' actions was always less important than awareness and necessary acceptance of their absolute power, especially in the case of Zeus, and this weighs the scales against the automatic assumption that an Athenian audience would have identified with Prometheus. But there are further points to be made concerning the political terms in which Zeus' power is described. How did an Athenian audience of the mid-fifth century BCE react to, for example, the idea of Zeus as an arbitrary tyrant? To what extent could Zeus' power and actions be subjected to the kind of criticism reserved for humans? Here the Io episode is relevant: the spotlight is put on Zeus' ruthlessness and cruelty, not only in what he actually does to Io and threatens to do to her father (664–7) but also by the way in which both the minimizing of the traditional role of Hera, Zeus' consort, in sending the gadfly which stung Io (702), and the minor role given to Argus (675–8), suggest that Aeschylus wished to put the responsibility largely on Zeus' shoulders. These are aspects which Paulin chooses to emphasize in his play, and they are not irrelevant to the Aeschylus *Prometheus Bound*.

We read in 848 that finally Zeus will come to Io 'with a gentle touch' and sire Epaphos, ancestor of future generations and especially of Prometheus' liberator. Attitudes to Zeus in *Prometheus Bound* cannot ignore the probability that, in the course of time, his role was perceived as less tyrannical (probably in *Prometheus Unbound*). We must be aware of this, and also of the fact that the play's original audience would have brought to the theatre their experience of Zeus in a variety of roles in the *polis*. Clearly Zeus was thought to have changed in the same way. Yet the fact remains that in no extant Greek tragedy (and certainly not in our only extant trilogy, the *Oresteia*) is Zeus portrayed in so unflattering a light. ♦

As I said at the beginning of this discussion, this is not a question which presents a clear answer. Aeschylus is presenting a conflict, not a resolution.

In considering this topic you might like to consider further the significance of the Chorus' commitment to Prometheus at the end of the play. In emphasizing *their* loyalty, as opposed to all the other apparent failures of commitment (not just of Zeus, but of Hephaestus and Oceanus too), is Aeschylus saying anything important about the Zeus/Prometheus conflict? Note especially 1066–7: 'I was taught to hate those who desert their friends; /and there is no infamy I more despise.' (Paulin's play emphasizes the final choice of the Chorus.) A possible way forward lies in the analysis of the political language of the play, and we shall return to this political dimension in Section 6 after you have read Sophocles' *Antigone* and *Oedipus the King*.

TMA02

2.7.2 Prometheus and mortals

Prometheus is a figure placed between the (other) gods and mortals – a mediator. We have seen how he handles his relationship with the gods, but how about his relationship with mortals? It is worth noting that the chief innovation of *Prometheus Bound* appears to be the important role given to Prometheus as a saviour of the human race, in defiance of Zeus. Indeed the relevance of the play to human concerns pervades the whole drama, yet only one character, Io, is not divine; and the preponderance of gods as characters in the play makes it unique in extant Greek drama.

How does Aeschylus make the play relevant to human concerns?

Discussion

On one level, the human dimension appears as peripheral to the struggle taking place, on behalf of mortals, by divinities. Yet we have already noted that mortals owe their original existence to an act done in defiance of Zeus; they were not, at least as far as Aeschylus is concerned, part of the original divine scheme of things – though they have obviously since become so. Through Prometheus they have been able to acquire the practical skills which ensure not only their survival but also progression to a high level of civilization. Human life is not, as for Hesiod, a pitiful side-show, but of central concern. And their survival has depended not on the Olympian gods, but on a hitherto obscure deity.

This optimistic view of human attainment was matched by a corresponding (Hesiodic) pessimism: 'Man is the dream of a shadow' says the mid-fifth-century Theban lyric poet Pindar, and his sentiment was a commonplace in Greek tragedy and elsewhere. Note that this estimate of humans is as Prometheus found them *before* he instructed them (444ff.). For the Chorus, he was wrong to give fire to creatures 'whose life is but a day' (253). Yet the play also celebrates the survival of the human race. It would not, I feel, be going too far to suggest that the celebration of Prometheus' gifts to mortals might also be seen as a celebration of their own ingenuity in making good use of their original instruction. They are both skilled and self-reliant and vulnerable to the power of the gods.

But where does that leave Prometheus? It is notable that although the play has only one human character, there is considerable emphasis upon minor deities whose lack of power to withstand Zeus puts them almost on a human level. This is especially true in the case of the Chorus who express 'human sentiments', especially in the third *stasimon* (887–906). It is from this identification that the ambivalence of Prometheus' own status arises: he is a god, but unable to defend himself against Zeus; he is isolated (this is expressed dramatically in his geographical remoteness) and seen as standing apart from the other gods (29, 37). There is also an ambivalence between Prometheus the all-knowing (101–2) and his ignorance of his ultimate fate (100–1). He has aspirations which identify him with humans, but unlike humans, he cannot die and put an end to his own suffering. This similarity and difference is most pointedly brought out in the Io episode, especially 753–4. When Io desires to commit suicide, Prometheus replies with poignant irony: 'Then you would find it hard to bear my agonies,/since I am fated not to die.'

If we accept as likely that an important aspect of the whole trilogy was the larger development of human–divine relationships, then *Prometheus Bound* in particular seems to be concerned to explore, in dramatic terms, the ambivalence of mortal status: in one aspect self-reliant, in another desperately dependent upon the whims of the gods for their further existence.

But is there also, perhaps, an ambivalence in mortal *attitude* to the gods? Is Aeschylus suggesting that mortals are aware that the gods, for all their power, lack certain qualities which humans can possess? ♦

2.8 Further Reading on *Prometheus Bound*

(For the general purpose of Further Reading, see the Course Guide.)

2.8.1 Primary sources

Of Aeschylus' plays, you have already read *The Persians* and will shortly be studying it in detail. If you wish to read further in Aeschylus, his *The Suppliants* is translated in the *Prometheus Bound* volume, pp.54–86 (the plot of this play is taken from an incident foretold by Prometheus in *Prometheus Bound* 853ff.). The *Oresteia*, Aeschylus' only trilogy and by general consent his masterpiece, is also translated in Penguin Classics by Robert Fagles. *Seven Against Thebes* (also in the *Prometheus Bound* volume) is a play from the Theban Cycle; you might like to read this after you have studied Sophocles' *Antigone* and *Oedipus the King*, both in order to compare poetic styles and also to look at treatments of different parts of the same story. You will find reference to this play in the sections which follow.

2.8.2 Secondary sources

1 GRIFFITH, M. (ed.) (1983) Aeschylus, *Prometheus Bound*, Cambridge University Press; available in paperback.

I have already referred to this book. It is the standard commentary on the Greek text, and, as such, contains much material relevant to students reading Greek. However there is a great deal in the notes, and especially the Introduction, which can be very useful to students reading the play in translation. Most of the points of importance and controversy which arose in our discussion above are summarized and discussed by Griffith with extensive reference to other bibliography.

2 CONACHER, D.J. (1980) *Aeschylus' Prometheus Bound: a literary commentary*, University of Toronto Press (available in paperback and, unlike Griffith above, quite likely to be stocked by a large public library).

A detailed discussion of every aspect of the play designed for a wide range of students (including, as the author explicitly states, those without Greek).

These two books both contain further bibliography. An additional study, well worth consulting, is:

3 TAPLIN, O. (1977) *The Stagecraft of Aeschylus*, Oxford University Press.

This book examines in exhaustive detail the staging of all the plays of Aeschylus, using all available evidence. It includes *Prometheus Bound* (pp.240–75). Although Taplin believes that the play is not by Aeschylus, partly on grounds of its dramatic atypicality, this does not affect the value of his survey, which is well worth reading. (There is untranslated Greek, but this is not a major barrier to understanding the main argument.) Note that Oliver Taplin is the author and presenter of Guest Lecture 1 (Cassette 9, Band 1).

3 *THE PERSIANS*

3.1 Introduction

It may initially seem rather strange to be reading what is probably Aeschylus' earliest extant play *after* his latest. The reason for this arrangement is, in the first instance, simply related to the development of A209 from A294; from a study point of view it made sense to add *The Persians* to the more detailed analysis of *Prometheus Bound* rather than vice versa. However, this ordering of the plays can be justified on other grounds also; having studied a play which perhaps relates in some of its details to the early Sophistic movement, in *The Persians* we return to the Persian Wars and expand the critical analysis of Aeschylus' treatment which was briefly introduced at the end of Block 1. In this way we will have studied in detail and consolidated a period of crucial importance for the understanding of events and ideas of the latter part of the century.

So, in this section we shall be reading *The Persians* (i) as a drama, in comparison with *Prometheus Bound*, and (ii) as a major early contribution to the cultural image of the Greeks and Persians in the fifth century.

First, listen to The Persians *on audio-cassette. Then reread Block 1, pp.26ff., and consider to what extent* The Persians *is a celebration of Athenian victory.*

PERFORMANCE

11

Discussion _____

I would say that the play is not straightforwardly celebratory. Aeschylus has chosen to recreate the events as seen through the eyes of the Persians – the enemy. Despite the cultural 'distancing' (see Block 1, 8), there is heroism on both sides; and the grief and fear of non-combatants, old men left at home and deserted wives with their children, is that of the Persians. Underlying the action throughout, and giving it direction, is a strong and pervasive theological dimension – the punishment by the gods of folly and overwhelming pride.

These two aspects, the focus on human suffering and on its causes, are what allows *The Persians* to transcend the simple celebration of Athenian victory. The Athenians are indeed praised as heroes who owe their success to personal bravery, a patriotic belief in their political system and a correct relationship with the gods; but in making their victory part of a larger human and theological scheme of things, Aeschylus (typically of Greek tragedians) avoids placing simple patriotism at the centre of the play. He requires in his audience a 'leap of sympathy', which embraces the defeated as well as themselves. ♦

Please now read through the play (Aeschylus, pp.122–52), and – if you have time – listen to it on audio-cassette. While doing so, give some thought (and make brief notes where appropriate) to the following topics, which I shall deal with in order:

- *staging and spectacle*

- *language and style*

- *dramatic structure and 'character'*

- *gods and humans (human perception of the role of the gods, and of human-divine relationships)*

- *presentation of Athens and Athenians.*

Then return to the discussion below. I do not (as I did with *Prometheus Bound*) work through the play in order; instead I highlight passages and lines under these five topics. (*NB* Location of line numbers in your translation: as with *Prometheus Bound*, you will need to count down or up from the lines indicated at the top of the page. In cases of doubt I shall make clear which line(s) I am referring to.)

3.2   Staging and spectacle

Look at the first five pages of The Persians. *Thinking (or referring) back to* Prometheus Bound, *what obvious structural difference can you see?*

Discussion _____

There is no Prologue: the play starts immediately with the Chorus entering in the *Parodos* (for this, and other technical terms, refer to Figure 4 on p.11). Absence of a Prologue may be an early feature (*The Suppliants*, pp.54–8, also has no Prologue, and in this respect was later seen as 'old-fashioned'). But here, in *The Persians*, it has the immediate effect of placing the Chorus (already prominent in the *orchestra*) at the centre of the play. Aeschylus also doubtless exploited the opportunity to use exotic, colourful 'Persian' dress for his Chorus members (as he also used outlandish-sounding but resonant Persian names: p.123). ♦

You will have noticed how prominent the Chorus is in this play, both in the *stasima* and in exchanges with the actors. Aeschylus has two actors (playing all the roles: see above, p.12) who occasionally engage in dialogue with each other (for example, pp.132, 142–3); but much more frequently the actors engage with the Chorus.

Think about how physical prominence is related to the Chorus' thematic importance in:

(i)   being guardians of the state, 'left in trust' (first line, p.122)

(ii) expressing the *emotional* reaction to events (for example, p.137)

(iii) broadening the theological picture (for example, p.125).

For the Chorus' role as 'visualizers' of distant events, see Section 3.3, 'Language and style', below.

Other elements of spectacle

Entrance of the Queen (p.127)

In your translation, the stage directions (modern, of course: see above, p.12, 3a) indicate the majestic spectacle of this entrance (from the door of the palace, represented by the *skene*). If you look back at the *parodos*, this moment obviously functions as the climax (lines 147–55, 'Look … favour fail'). But, typically of this play, confident display overlies fear and apprehension in Atossa's speech (lines 156ff.). There is also a visual and dramatic contrast with Atossa's later entrance (p.139), where the translator's stage direction 'alone' is a reasonable inference from 609.

Appearance of the ghost of Darius (p.141)

This would obviously be a striking spectacle, however contrived. (The discussion above, p.13, warns that the complexity of stage-effects would be limited by physical circumstances of presentation: forget 'trapdoors' and the like!) Once again, as with Atossa above, the entrance is elaborately prepared by the Chorus' 'summoning' the ghost (pp.140–1).

Entrance of Xerxes (p.147)

In contrast this, the most important entrance, happens without warning, though in a sense the whole play has been building up to it. The conclusion is a violently emotional *kommos* between Xerxes and Chorus, in which sorrow dissolves gradually into inarticulate expressions of grief (p.151) to which the printed text hardly does justice (listen to Audio-Cassette 1, Band 2, Section 1, on expressions of grief in Greek). O. Taplin (1977, p.128) plausibly suggests that this final *kommos* would be best played if Xerxes were to join the Chorus in the *orchestra*, since nothing in the text suggests that they are separated (it is quite probable that the areas of stage and *orchestra* were much less clearly separated at this early date than they appear in all the remains of theatres that we see today; see TV3).

3.3 Language and style

As in *Prometheus Bound*, the play divides into two basic types of language and style:

(i) the lyric (the Chorus *stasimon* and the final *kommos* with Xerxes). This is associated with song and dance (see above, p.11, Section 1).

(ii) speech and dialogue (for example, between Chorus and Atossa).

As in *Prometheus Bound*, this distinction can usually be roughly detected from the different lengths of lines in the translation (see above, p.10).

Using your knowledge of Prometheus Bound, *consider for a moment how these two elements are used in the play. In other words, what types of expression are there? (Look at, for example, pp.122–6 and 133–7.)*

Discussion _____

(i) The Chorus provides the most obvious examples of elevated language. The *parodos* (pp.122–7) illustrates their two most prominent aims. First, to give the heroic 'roll-call' of Persian fighters (p.123: Aeschylus exploits exotic and outlandish names. Remember the same characteristic with Io's wanderings in *Prometheus Bound*?). Their second aim is to articulate the apprehension of the outcome (for example, p.125). The chorus helps to 'universalize' the events – to put them in the 'larger scheme of things' – and at the same time to present them vividly to the audience (for example, p.138).

Perhaps even more than in *Prometheus Bound*, we encounter Aeschylus' daring and colourful use of language, especially simile and metaphor (see especially p.125, 'For when armies ... fear can sway', lines 87ff; and 'Yet, while Heaven ... death will keep', lines 94ff.). Aeschylus' high-flown lyric style, which has had an influence on poets of the early and mid-twentieth century (Eliot, Yeats), was regarded in the fifth century BCE as his trademark, and was effectively parodied by Aristophanes in his comedy *Frogs* (406 BCE).

(ii) *As in* Prometheus Bound, there are speeches and exchanges between characters. Note, however, two distinct elements:

(a) the exchanges: unlike those in *Prometheus Bound*, these are not competitive or argumentative. The point of *stichomythia* is usually to elicit information (pp.129–30, Atossa from the Chorus; pp.142–3, Darius from Atossa). Or at least this is the ostensible purpose. What other dramatic function might these exchanges fulfil?

(b) the Messenger Speech (pp.130–37): this is a key element in most tragedies. *The Persians* has one of the most elaborate. Aeschylus uses the traditional 'messenger function' – whether performed by a messenger or other character (for example, Io in *Prometheus Bound*) – to bring momentous and often violent events before the audience by eye-witness description. This virtuoso speech scarcely needs comment in this context, except for us to notice that it is clearly structured into sections (articulated by interjections and questions from Atossa and Chorus), in which the Messenger passes from general comment, through a roll-call of prominent Persian dead, to the three narratives of: the Battle of Salamis (pp.133–4), its conclusion (pp.135–6), and the Persian retreat (pp.136–7). The tension is maintained by the Messenger's assurance that there is worse to come (p.135, lines 435–6). ◆

Note that, in Aeschylus, passages of elevated poetic description are not confined to the 'chorus' elements.

3.4 Dramatic structure and 'character'

Consider the following questions for a moment. (i) Who is the central character of the play? (ii) How is this character portrayed?

Discussion _____

(i) This was not a problem with *Prometheus Bound*, but here it might be thought an ambiguous question: it depends on what you mean by 'central' (and, incidentally, shows how much 'character' and dramatic structure are intertwined). Who dominates visually? (The Chorus, after whom the play is named.) Which character apart from the Chorus spends longest on the stage? (Atossa.) Which character represents the theological argument most clearly? (Darius.) But what I mean by 'central' here is: which character is the play about, the character whose actions, personality and fate, motivate and propel the plot? The answer surely is Xerxes.

(ii) In the starkest contrast to *Prometheus Bound*, where Prometheus is dragged onto the stage at the beginning and stays throughout, Xerxes appears only in the last scene (pp.147–52). Yet he is the unifying element, in the sense that the play is about him and his pride, which leads to his downfall (see especially p.138, lines 548ff., with the accusation against Xerxes repeated twice for emphasis). The other characters in the play all relate to some aspect of Xerxes' situation: Atossa in her maternal fear for her son's safety (p.128); the Chorus as noble Persians representing his kingdom and its suffering (pp.137–9); the messenger, describing the authoritarian arrogance leading to military defeat (p.133); Darius drawing the contrast (historically much exaggerated) with his own wise rule (pp.143–4).

As with other Greek tragedies, character tends to define itself in terms of dramatic function, and there are limitations on the development of character as we know it. (See above, p.13, on the significance of stylization, use of masks, etc.) ◆

3.5 Gods and humans

Relationships between gods and humans are very important in this play. First, look back at Prometheus Bound *(and, if you need to, Section 2.7 above) and decide, in a couple of sentences, what the position of the gods was in that play.*

Discussion _____

Prometheus Bound was, of course, set in the far distant mythical past, and it was principally about the strife between gods. The play – through its principal character, Prometheus – conveyed a questioning and often critical attitude towards Zeus' authority. As far as mortals are concerned, note the remark on p.34: '...the ambivalence of mortal status: in one aspect self-reliant, in another desperately dependent upon the whims of the gods for their further existence.' ◆

Now consider The Persians. *Please read two passages: (i) p.125, line 80 ('From the darkness ...') to p.126, line 105 ('hempen cords'); and (ii) p.145, top of page to line 832 ('rash attempts', near the bottom of the page). What do these passages tell us about the presentation of the gods in the play?*

Discussion _____

(i) There is a clear movement from the irresistible power of the Persian army (first two stanzas: *strophe* and *antistrophe*) to the will of the gods, which tricks the overconfident ('immortal guile', 'net' and 'trap': second *strophe* and *antistrophe*). And this downfall is associated with deluded attempts to take to the *sea* (final lines of the passage on p.126). The theological dimension is firmly and crucially anchored to historical reality. In the whole enterprise Xerxes is fatally overreaching himself by meeting the Greeks on *their* element, water.

See also Darius' speech on p.143, and the attempt to overpower Poseidon, god of the sea, 11 lines from the bottom; note also the bridge of boats across the Hellespont (p.124, lines 69–74) and Darius' horrified reaction (p.142, lines 721–6).

(ii) Darius' speech (p.145) adds two important aspects. *First*, it suggests the degree to which Xerxes' downfall is deserved: his downfall is a punishment for wanton destruction (lines 809–11), arrogance and boastfulness (lines 824–5), and is also described as the outcome of pride (*hybris*, line 819, 'for pride will blossom') which 'ripens into infatuation' (820). The Greek word *ate* (infatuation) is here the same as 'Delusion', which the Chorus used in the *parodos* (p.125); and delusion leads to destruction.

Secondly the violence is not just – or even primarily – against persons, but against the statues and temples of the gods (lines 809–11). So Xerxes' action is a direct attack on the gods through their images and dwellings on earth (sacrilege), and against their temples etc. as a symbol of the unified Greek race. (For this latter theme, see *ST* 13(k), pp.25–6, where Herodotus presents the Athenians stating their need to avenge the Persian burning and destruction of the temples of the Greek gods.) See also the rallying cry of the Greeks as related by the Messenger on p.134 (lines 400ff.), which includes the 'tombs of your ancestors' and the 'temples of your gods'. Throughout the play, patriotism is closely linked with human–divine relationships. ◆

The movement (arrogance→delusion→destruction) is reflected in the whole play; for example, in the *parodos* where heroic optimism alternates with apprehension (see the common motif of the weighing-scale, p.132, line 346). Aeschylus uses this technique to generate suspense, especially by foreshadowing bad news; for example, Atossa's dream (p.128) and Darius' prophecy (p.145). He also uses language ambiguously to generate suspense: for example, line 9 (p.122) where 'left home' has, in Greek, strong overtones of 'gone' or 'destroyed', echoed in 'departed' at line 547 (p.138).

Note also how this pervasive movement (good fortune→destruction) is used by the messenger twice in his speech: (i) Salamis (p.133), where Xerxes' numerical superiority is totally undermined by the gods, and (ii) Xerxes' retreat (p.136), where joyful hope at the freezing of the ice to allow passage turns to despair in the face of the implacable gods' action in melting it. The Persian prayers were not answered.

We also see the operation of a key aspect of Greek perception of the gods, namely 'double-determination'. Xerxes' downfall occurs on two levels: he causes it himself through his arrogance and pride, but the gods also act to destroy him. As Darius says (p.143, line 743): 'But heaven takes part, for good or ill, with man's own zeal.'

The Persians does not, as *Prometheus Bound* does, question or make a problem of divine activity. We see, rather, the acceptance of divine authority and the highlighting of the terrible consequences of the flouting of divine will.

3.6 Presentation of Athens and Athenians

This historical bias of *The Persians* has already been mentioned in Block 1. Athens is given perhaps excessive prominence over other Greek states (though the text also refers frequently to 'Hellas' and 'Hellene', for example, lines 790, 826).[1] We have also mentioned Darius' polarized view of the distinction between the 'golden age' of his reign contrasted with that of his son Xerxes (p.144; and see the Chorus on p.146). The play barely mentions that it was Darius who initiated hostilities against the Greeks and was defeated at Marathon (see *WA*, pp.11–12). (But see also p.129, line 236, which makes it clear that the Persians have met the Greeks in battle before.) Yet Aeschylus' isolating of Xerxes in his folly, and the creation of an illusory Persian 'golden age', have the *dramatic* effect of polarizing right and wrong. The blame is entirely on Xerxes.

The Persians, while concentrating on the defeated, also refers to the victors. Look for a moment at some relevant passages:

(i) p.128, lines 212–14 ('If my son conquers ... Persia's king')

(ii) p.129, middle of page ('But tell me ... they destroyed', bottom of the page)

(iii) p.132, line 348–52 (bottom of page)

(iv) p.133, lines 365–9 ('Then he sent ... dazed his mind'), and p.134, lines 400–2 ('Forward, you sons ... now fight!').

What do these tell you about Aeschylus' portrayal of Athens and Athenians, contrasted with the Persians?

Discussion

Aeschylus' portrayal is strongly patriotic, with considerable political emphasis. Note the emphasis on *political* contrast: the Athenians do not fight at the dictates of a master but (by implication) through the desire to defend their country: see (ii). In (i), Xerxes – by contrast – is a tyrant who is not 'answerable' (p.128, line 213, where the Greek word *hypeuthunos* indicates the *euthune* or audit, which outgoing state officials had to submit to at Athens; also used of Zeus in *Prometheus Bound*, line 324).

The Greek also adds the word *polis*: so Xerxes is not answerable to a 'city state'. The contrast between tyrannical violence and the 'democratic' self-discipline of the *polis* is further illustrated by the behaviour of Xerxes and the Greeks before Salamis (iv), where the former exerts discipline by threatening his captains with execution, whereas the latter are motivated by their patriotic instincts as Greeks. The political merits of the Athenians are emphasized – as so often in Greek – by polar contrast.[2]

The other point, finally, concerns the way in which Aeschylus refers to the Athenian state; (iii) has been mentioned in Block 1 as a neat bypassing of the burning and destruction of Athens by the Persians. Yet, as Block 1 also makes clear, the messenger is not just avoiding facts that are uncomfortable for the Athenians, but is emphasizing in line 349 that while Athenian men survive, so will the city – irrespective of what may happen to the physical remains. Despite the element of patriotic exaggeration here, the equation of the city with its citizens (and remember that Herodotus and Thucydides usually say 'The Athenians' and not 'Athens') is a potent image, which you will meet again shortly when reading Sophocles' *Antigone*. ♦

---

[1] E. Hall, in the Introduction to her edition of the play (see Further Reading at the end of Section 3), suggests (p.12) that the play is 'a nascent expression of the very tension between Panhellenic ideals and Athenian, imperial ideology, which was to inform historiography, tragedy, and comedy throughout the fifth century'.

[2] The contrast would be even sharper if one assumed, with E. Hall (note on 374-83), that 'in good order' and 'obediently' at 370 (translation) referred to Greeks rather than, as Vellacott translates, to Persians. The Greek is not clear here, however.

3.7 Further questions

In Section 6 there will be some general comparisons between *The Persians* and other tragedies that you will read in Block 2. Here, to conclude, are a few questions to be considering:

1 How would you explain the differences in attitudes to the gods in *The Persians* and *Prometheus Bound*? Some distinctions may be relevant: *Prometheus Bound* is generally thought to be part of a trilogy and we don't get the full theological picture (see above, p.32); *The Persians* is our earliest extant tragedy (472 BCE) whereas *Prometheus Bound* is probably Aeschylus' last play (or even written by someone else after his death – late 450s or 440s BCE) with the discernible influence of early sophistic thought – 'battles of ideas' etc. Yet do these reservations explain everything? Are we perhaps looking at two *complementary* aspects of Athenian attitudes towards the gods, dramatically portrayed?

2 Could both plays be described as 'political' or 'patriotic'? And in what senses? In what ways do they differ in this respect? We have just considered *The Persians* in this context (Section 3.6). Looking back at *Prometheus Bound*, consider how these words might be applied. (Look at what might be *implied* as well as explicitly said.) What resonances might an audience detect in either play? (See *Prometheus Bound*, p.32, and Section 2.7 above; and don't forget TV1 *Seize the Fire*.)

3 Aristotle the philosopher, writing his *Poetics* about 150 years after Aeschylus, describes 'pity' and 'fear' as the proper emotions to be generated by the events of tragedy. Allowing that it is not clear whether Aristotle was simply generalizing from his experience of Greek tragedy or constructing an ideal, or both, to what extent do you think that *The Persians* generates pity and fear? And in what way? (Note what we said at the beginning concerning the fact that the catastrophe being viewed is happening to *enemies*: see the discussion on p.36.) And in what proportion? If you have time, please do the same exercise with *Prometheus Bound*.

4 Finally, looking back to Block 1, Section 7, decide in what specific ways you consider that *The Persians* contributes to the Athenian's sense of their own identity. (This is a recap exercise: consider different areas – moral, political, theological.)

3.8 Further Reading on *The Persians*

BROADHEAD, H.D. (1960) *The Persae of Aeschylus*, Cambridge (until recently the standard scholarly edition of the play, with a useful introduction).

GREEN, R. and HANDLEY, E. (1994) *Images of the Greek Theatre*, British Museum Press.

HALL, E. (1996) *The Persians, Text, Translation and Commentary*, Warminster, Aris and Philips (the most recent scholarly edition).

PODLECKI, A. (1966) *The Political Background of Aeschylus' Tragedy*, Ann Arbor (see Chapter 2, 'The Persians').

TAPLIN, O. (1977) *The Stagecraft of Aeschylus*, Oxford.

4 ANTIGONE

4.1 Sophocles and the Theban Plays

Just as we relish the fact that Aeschylus fought at the battle of Marathon, and wished to be remembered for that alone (see *WA* H.I.13), so we have a few glimpses of information about Sophocles (for example, *ST* 24(a)) which are tantalizingly insufficient, and from which we try to reconstruct a living picture of the man. One established fact is that he was chosen as one of the generals in 441 BCE (perhaps because of the success of *Antigone* at the Dionysia that year): he took part in the expedition against Samos, and was sent by Pericles on a diplomatic mission to Chios and Lesbos. There were other civic duties and appointments later. This serves to indicate that, unlike a nineteenth-century 'artist', he saw no opposition between his theatrical calling and serving his city by holding high office. This experience could not be literally realized in his plays, which all have mythological subject-matter; but it should make us consider that his 'ruling-class' characters may be based, to a certain extent, upon observation, and that he would be unlikely to portray the ruler of a state as a simple 'cartoon' character, or be opposed to the exercise of authority. These last two points should be remembered when we come to the play of *Antigone*.

The developments in Greek drama during the fifth century might well be compared to the 'improvements' in television drama over the past thirty-five years. How dated the plays of the 1960s have become – the famous 'realism' of *Z-Cars*, for example, would seem so glaringly 'theatrical' now. Over a longer period great changes took place in the Greek theatre, which was open to rapid innovation at that time. Sophocles increased the number of speaking actors on stage from two to three, moving the drama away from a kind of oratorio with two solo recitative or declamatory parts – think back to *Prometheus Bound* – towards scenes of confrontation and intervention by more rounded 'characters', pushing the Chorus into the background. (I exaggerate a point which I cannot prove in order to make you see what 'increasing the actors from two to three' actually does in the theatre; but you will find there are parts of *Antigone* in which only two actors have important scenes to play.) Sophocles is also said to have introduced painted scenery. He was famous as a 'teacher of the Chorus', and wrote a *Treatise on the Chorus*. In all he is reckoned to have been the author of over a hundred plays, many of which were awarded the first prize: it is important to note that he seems to have abandoned the practice of producing them in connected trilogies. It is difficult to prove these statements, because only seven of his plays survive in their entirety.

Now you might have expected from the title of your set book – *The Three Theban Plays* – that what is between the covers amounts to a trilogy. This is not the case, but for another reason than that suggested in the preceding paragraph: the three plays were written at widely separated intervals. *Antigone* seems to be the earliest, *Oedipus the King* may have a reference to the Athenian plague of 429 BCE, and we know that *Oedipus at Colonus* was first put on stage in 401 BCE, after Sophocles had died. *Your set book therefore places them in this order.* But note that when they are presented on the modern stage or on television, they are usually played as a trilogy in the order of the mythical story of Oedipus and his children.

4.2 The House of Oedipus

The story of Oedipus may be well known to you, although there is a full account on pages 27–29 of your set book. *Please read this now. If you have already read it, you should still refer to the section as necessary.* Meanwhile, in anticipation of the play *Antigone*, I would like to recall the main points of the story as it is retold in *The Three Theban Plays*, as if from the point of view of Antigone herself.

In *Oedipus the King* we encounter the mature Oedipus, king of the city of Thebes, which is in the grip of a plague. The city is polluted and Oedipus is determined to find the source of the pollution. In doing so he discovers his own history. His father Laius and his mother Jocasta had been warned by Apollo that their son would kill his father: Oedipus had therefore been cast out of the city as a baby and his feet maimed. A shepherd had saved his life. He was brought up in Corinth, as the son of the royal family of that city. On hearing a similar oracle from Apollo – that he was destined to kill his father – he had made a journey to Thebes to escape his fate. On the way he unwittingly killed his true father in what seemed to him a needlessly violent encounter. In Thebes he solved the riddle of the Sphinx, and, again unwittingly, married his biological mother. After these facts have been revealed Oedipus blinds himself. His daughters, Antigone and Ismene, only appear in this play as small children in a pathetic farewell scene as Oedipus leaves the city.

In *Oedipus at Colonus* we find that Oedipus has become an aged wanderer, and also an important cult-figure, almost a 'saint', whose sufferings have in some sense redeemed him. He is led to the territory of Athens; he repulses various messengers from the contending factions at Thebes, and dies mysteriously in a sacred grove, rewarding Athens with the promise of a victory which would be connected with his burial-place. In this play Antigone appears as the faithful guide of the blind man. (Note that in *Seven against Thebes* by Aeschylus, the two sons of Oedipus, Eteocles and Polynices, do battle for the city. This is a good example of an 'old-fashioned' play, which you can find in the same Penguin volume as *Prometheus Bound*. One can assume that the folk-tale legend of the two fighting brothers – compare Balin and Balan in Malory's *Morte d'Arthur* – and the magical number of the Seven Champions who assault the city would be as commonplace as Noah's Ark to ourselves. A possibly spurious ending to the play introduces Antigone and Ismene discussing the burial of their brothers.)

Finally, in *Antigone*, which begins after the events of *Seven Against Thebes*, the city has come under the control of Creon, Jocasta's brother, as Oedipus' male heirs are both dead. Creon's decision not to allow burial of the corpse of Polynices, who had organized the attack on the city, leads to the main conflict of the play. Antigone does bury her brother, is condemned to death by Creon, and this, in turn, leads to the destruction of his own family.

The earliest known reference to the story of Oedipus is in Homer, but there is no mention of Antigone. Unlike the Hesiodic myth of Prometheus, there is no extant early source (prior to Sophocles) which gives us a saga or epic narrative of the primary material which Sophocles might have used.

As you know from the general discussion of Greek tragedy (Section 1.4), the Greek dramatists seem to have had a free hand – provided they did not offend credibility or go against the generally available telling of the legend. In this case it may well be that Sophocles, who was famous for being faithful to Homer, knowing that there was no mention in his authoritative source of Oedipus' daughters, took this as his justification for continuing the story of Aeschylus' *Seven Against Thebes* in his own way.

4.3 The play

Now read the play through quickly.

As with Prometheus Bound, *you should try to imagine a performance while you read. You should use the Performance Cassette of* Antigone *(Cassette 7) in the same way as you did with* Prometheus Bound *(Cassette 6). See p.17 for instructions on how to use the Performance Cassette. Then proceed to 4.3.1.*

PERFORMANCE
7

4.3.1 Preliminary questions

I should like you, at this stage, to look over these questions and the notes attached to them. The commentary which follows at 4.4 is in close focus on the text, and therefore tends to proceed line-by-line, but you should have these general questions at the back of your mind. Some of them will receive attention in the general essays which follow the commentary, but not all.

Greek drama/staging etc.

a) *Can you describe and locate the broad divisions of the text (as you did with* Prometheus Bound *in Section 1.5)?*

The Greek names will be used in the commentary (see the table of terms, Figure 4 above): these are more precise than *Act* and *Scene* which remind one of Shakespeare and the later Western theatre.

b) *How does the Chorus function in this play?*

Is the *content* of the choruses dramatically appropriate? Sophocles seems to have been particularly famous for his choruses during his life-time.

c) *What are the differences between this play and Aeschylus'* Prometheus Bound*?*

An obvious one is that gods and demigods do not appear in *Antigone*. Nevertheless the characters, though human, are from the heroic age. You know that Sophocles increased the number of speaking actors on the stage from two to three: how does this work out? You might consider whether it adds to the complexity of the drama, and gives an opportunity for other kinds of discourse than a simple debate or question and answer.

d) *If the gods do not appear, how are their views made known?*

This is quite a difficult question which you could decide is invalid. We are told by human beings about the gods' views, but couldn't this be as a justification of their own actions? What about Tiresias and his effect on Creon?

Tragedy

Rather than try to formulate general views on tragedy on the basis of two plays, consider:

a) *The 'tragedy of Antigone'*

Is she credible? Is she consistent? Is she an example of moral heroism? Or does she push one idea too far, i.e. beyond the virtue of moderation? You may know/care to note that elsewhere, for example in *Ajax* and *Trachiniae*, Sophocles chooses extreme situations, and is interested in how people behave under the stress of those situations.

b) *The 'tragedy of Creon'*

(He is on stage at the end of the play, whereas Antigone has disappeared from our view well before that.) What is there to be said for him? Does he have an inner life, or is he just a spokesman for a point of view? You would expect him to have no 'tragedy' if he is simply a foil to Antigone.

c) *The 'tragedy of Antigone and Creon'*

Are they both involved equally, on opposite sides?

d) *The 'tragic pattern' of Sophocles' plays (if you know others)*

There is often said to be a 'clock wound-up ready to strike' or an 'enclosing net in which the doomed bull-like male is enmeshed' (these remarks refer to *Oedipus the King* and *Ajax* respectively).

e) *How others, i.e. Haemon and Eurydice, are involved and 'have to die' because of the activities of Antigone and Creon.*

Is the tragedy a kind of multiple accident which involves the innocent bystanders in the final catastrophe?

Moral ideas

a) *'The duties owed to the state are opposed to the duties owed to religion'*

i.e. You can't render unto Caesar and unto God simultaneously. Will this do?

b) *'The state's laws are opposed to the individual citizen's moral judgements'*

i.e. Is the play 'about Heseltine and Sarah Tisdall' as the actors performing the BBC version, discussed in TV2, thought it was in 1986? (Sarah Tisdall leaked information about the arrival of Cruise missiles, because she felt the state should not withhold such important facts from its citizens. Michael Heseltine was Minister of Defence at the time.)

c) *Is 'polis' (state) opposed to 'oikos' (kin)?*

Do we have a clash of two systems of morality which are self-contained, and exist as it were 'in parallel universes' in Greek society? (N.B. This historical view of the moral problems might detract from the universality perceived by the BBC actors in (b) above.)

d) *Is there such a thing as too extreme or too provocative goodness?*

If you know *King Lear*, compare Cordelia's role in provoking Lear's anger; you don't of course have to agree with this interpretation of Shakespeare's play.

e) *Is drama correctly seen as a 'school of morality with examples of virtue and vice?'*

Many have wished this were so, and disapproved of 'gratuitous sex and violence', etc. etc. – but perhaps the enduring interest of a drama like this is that it sets out moral problems which are *insoluble*, i.e. the play would be boring if there were no puzzle about it. (You will find in the Introduction to the set book, pp.36–7, that Brecht produced a version in which Creon was equivalent to Hitler. What does this do to the play?)

f) *Is this a subversive text?*

Quite an interesting question to explore if we knew enough about the society of Athens at the time. Do you think the audience applauded Antigone? If so, what might this imply?

Now read the play slowly and carefully, using the commentary on the following pages, and the notes at the end of your set book. At this stage you should also use the Performance Cassette (Cassette 7).

PERFORMANCE

7

Figure 8 Still from Bertold Brecht's production of *Antigone* in Hölderlin's version, in Chur, February 1948, showing Tiresias (right) confronting Creon. The actors sat on benches in the background, and came forward into a space marked out by horses' heads on poles. Set designs by Caspar Neher. (Photograph by courtesy of the Archiv of Theatervereins, Chur.)

4.4   Commentary

Page and line numbers refer to Robert Fagles' translation in Sophocles, *The Three Theban Plays*, Penguin Classics, 1984. The line numbers used in this commentary are those by the *side* of the translation; those at the top of each page refer to the lines of the original Greek text.

p.57   Characters
Ismene is also a daughter of the incestuous relationship between Oedipus and his mother, Jocasta. Creon is Jocasta's brother.

p.59   Stage directions
Not in the Greek, of course. Supplied by the translator. But useful.

Lines 1–116: Prologue (2 actors)

'The royal house of Thebes'
Because it was the standard Greek theatre back-drop (see *WA* 7.50–51), the *skene* building of wood (later of stone) was read as the outer wall of a house. In any case most action in a hot country takes place in the street. Nevertheless, there is the point that the palace would be *full of spies*, see line 23.

'*Enter* ANTIGONE'
We have to assume that the audience would know who Antigone was, either from their general knowledge of mythology or perhaps from Aeschylus' *Seven against Thebes* or other (lost) plays which told the preceding part of the story. Sophocles has to establish in the first speeches who the two masked figures are – notice the names clearly in the first line of each first speech – and their relationship.

1	At first this seems one of the strangest opening lines of any play, which reads literally in the Greek 'O (of one kin/common) true sisterly *head* of Ismene', which is not easy to render equivalently. The point is that there is no other family like that of Oedipus and his wife/mother (Antigone is saying, 'I recognize you as special and unique'), and also that, with the deaths of Eteocles and Polynices, there is nobody else left of the set of four siblings, only *'the two of us'* (line 4). Without Ismene, Antigone is alone.
2–8	In spite of the high morality my 'preliminary questions' insisted upon, the Greek myths were originally told by people who believed firmly in the fact that the children inherit the sins of the fathers. To a fifth-century Greek audience there would be no doubt that the curse on the house of Labdacus (Oedipus' grandfather) had to run its course, regardless of human intervention (see lines 61–9). Keeping this in mind you could say that Antigone's apparent paranoia or 'persecution complex' is not internal to her character (as in Freud), but she is acting out the part of a doomed woman (i.e. motivated externally by the gods). The play explores these interpretations of her character and behaviour: neither of the interpretations is ruled out.
8–13	The latest news, as yet unknown to Ismene, is to be conveyed to us. Already, this first speech contains the germ of the play – the relationship of siblings, the curse of the gods, the decree of the Commander of the State.
9	Commander = *strategos*, usually translated 'general'. Remember that Sophocles had been a general and that Pericles' title was 'general' at Athens.
12–13	In his book *Reading Greek Tragedy* (Cambridge University Press, 1986), Simon Goldhill centres his reading of the play on the recurrent opposition of enemies (*ekhthroi*) and friends (*philoi*). 'Friends', of course, includes relations. See Section 2.7.1 above.
14–21	Ismene supplies the necessary preliminary information before Antigone's crowning and crucial revelation of the decree's content. It still seems a little odd that the events she refers to *are those of the preceding twenty-four hours*; it sounds as if she is thinking of a long way back when she contrasts 'just this very night'.
26–36	Creon's decree is often discussed in terms of parallels from contemporary history. It is certainly true that the Athenians denied burial on Attic soil to people guilty of treason and, when public indignation was aroused, were capable of acts which went beyond the legal limit. For example, there was a tradition of which the Athenians were rather proud that in the Persian Wars the Assembly stoned to death a citizen who had quite legally *spoken* in favour of surrender (Demosthenes 18, 204). But we must bear in mind that the decree is part of a story which is taking place in 'pre-historic' or 'heroic' times so that fifth-century examples are not necessarily relevant. When reading the story of Little Red Riding Hood to children, we do not feel the need to explain that if wolves still existed in the wild in England, they would be a protected species. Secondly, what is important here is that Creon goes against public sentiment. Thirdly, if Creon's decree, leaving the dead unburied, presents no problem to the audience, the whole point of the tragedy would disappear.
37–8	'for you and me', because it is the duty of the women of the *oikos* to bury the family dead. If you think Antigone is already imagining herself the victim of a 'persecution complex', you are not necessarily wrong though.
45	'or a coward': Ismene is already 'put down', before she can speak.

47–116   The points of this exchange to note:

- a) It has simply not occurred to Ismene to do anything (51).

- b) She cannot *imagine* an action against the law of the city (54).

- c) Her only explanation of this is that Antigone who has always been self-willed has no sense (58 and 60–81).

- d) The laws of the city are all-powerful (70–73).

- e) Women must not fight with men (74–5) .

- f) Antigone seems to really want to go it alone anyway (81–5).

- g) She is in some sense 'in love' with death (86–90).

- h) The laws of the gods cannot be dishonoured. 'An outrage sacred to the gods!' seems to encapsulate what the play is to be about – the conflict between the law of the city and the law of the gods (88, 91–2).

- i) There is at least sense in keeping the burial secret (98–9)

- j) Antigone commands the 'love' of her sister nevertheless, and presumably 'ones' includes and pre-signifies Haemon (116).

Lines 117–179: Parodos – The entry of the Chorus

'The old citizens'

Besides choruses of 'women', as in *Prometheus Bound*, the tragedians often use a chorus of old men ('elders').

What might be the dramatic reasons in this case?

Discussion

a) The young men are still in the army, pursuing the Argive attackers.

b) Younger people would be more inclined to interfere with the action, instead of commenting on it.

c) The old can comment from a wealth of experience, and while this is not a democracy, their approval seems necessary to Creon's kingship (175–9). Is this a reflection of democratic ideas which would be more at home in historical Athens than pre-historic Thebes?

d) It might be argued that their counsels will be moderate, but not necessarily to be taken as morally *central* (though the Greeks believed in moderation). ◆

Your edition usefully explains the narrative element of the Chorus (p.396).

117–20   Note the need to establish the passing of time, from night to dawn. The action will take place in a single day.

120–72   Consider the patriotism of the lines, and how the association of Polynices with the Argive enemy prepares us for the general support the Chorus give to Creon at first. But the Chorus are not *personally* *vindictive* against Polynices.

140   Notice that this could, with irony, apply to others than the Argives.

171–2   The lines serve to remind us that the play itself is performed at a festival honouring Dionysos.

173–4   Creon is now regarded as king which he justifies in lines 192–3 (see the genealogy on p.425 of the set text) as the nearest male relative.

Lines 179–376: First Episode (2 actors and the leader of the Chorus)

What do you make of Creon's speech (179–235)? Is there another view than that of the Introduction to your set book, pages 37–41? At this point, before attempting to answer this question, you should listen to the Interactive Cassette, Cassette 1, Band 3.

INTERACTIVE 1

Discussion

The Interactive Cassette discussion considers the implications of alternative views. To me, Creon's first speech radiates – underneath the official sentiments – insecurity, the need of a jack-in-office for 'respect', the wish of a new ruler to 'get a grip on things'. In other words, the new ruler casts around for an action which costs nothing but shows his power, literally 'hitting a man when he is down'. To me, the first action of the 'statesman' is cruel and mean. What do you think? You could say that Creon is a limited but dependable military man who has to sort out the mess left by Oedipus and his children. The speech was admired by Demosthenes in the fourth century BCE (see the Introduction to the set text, p.35) and he quotes 194–213 against his opponent Aeschines to remind him of the proper duties of a citizen (though Demosthenes' approval does not extend to the character of Creon himself). ◆

229–31   To refuse burial is to deny the spirit entry to Hades. For other points see *WA* 4.77.

236–40   Is there an ironic edge to these remarks of the Chorus? You could say that the leader (a) has not expected this; (b) hints that this is rather a petty use of the newly acquired 'power'; (c) does not (superstitiously?) even mention the corpse of Polynices.

244–6   Here again, the leader is puzzled at being summoned out specially, but almost to no purpose.

248–314 The sentry. Off-stage events have to be narrated by a messenger. See how this basic idea is improved by making the actual sentry take this job. His fear is parodied into comic relief. Most of the narrative is clear, but notice the reference to 'dogs and wild beasts' (293–4) casually echoing Creon's words (230).

317–44   Here again, notice Creon's insincerity emerging in all this, especially 328–32. The burial has become 'politicized'. We are no longer concerned with burial customs, but with an issue constantly enacted in reality in modern times. Refraining from burial is a kind of loyalty test, like avoiding a leak of information, or suppressing a 'banned' book.

356–75   Notice that even in fear of death, the sentry has little real respect for Creon, who flounders about, unable either to dismiss the sentry or, on the other hand, to arrest him, so that he finally has to make an exit himself. In fact, the sentry gets away scot-free.

Lines 376–424: First Stasimon

377–416 The Chorus sing the praise of Man, and his ingenuity, in terms that make us think of the Bible ('What is man?') and *Hamlet* ('What a piece of work is man'). It could be argued that this is a set-piece song only remotely relevant to the play, and it seems perverse to suggest that they are 'thinking of the daring and ingenuity of the person who gave Polynices' body symbolic burial' (note on p.397 of the set text). The Chorus stress that although Man seems to have tamed the natural world, Death is a mystery which Man will never conquer (lines 404–5) – and must therefore be respected. 'Inhumanity' will be cast out of the city; 'whoever does such things' refers to the person who has broken the ' laws of the land', but ironically prefigures Creon's fate. It is an illusion, say the Chorus, to pretend that Man is safe enough to defy the gods if he breaks those laws which define his 'humanity'.

416   The stasimon concludes here; in 417–24 the Leader alone probably speaks and knits in the song to the action. In the end the Chorus were wrong: it was a woman, not a man, who has defied Creon (this point is much clearer in the Greek).

Lines 425–655: Second Episode (3 actors and the leader; the same actor plays the sentry and returns as Ismene: see *WA* 7.51.)

425–94   Here again fulfilling two functions, the sentry is necessary as messenger to relate the action off-stage, but is also part of the present action as Antigone's guard.

463   The strange whirlwind can be taken as assistance from the gods.

479   This time the burial-rite is fully enacted.

499–524 There has been a good deal of reference to Zeus, under his different aspects. This time it is Zeus as the guardian of religious laws who is invoked. The Justice (who dwells with Hades) *positively* commands funeral observances. It is also the *woman's* duty to perform the funeral rites (520). But the speech ends with unnecessarily cheeky provocation, perhaps implying that the daughter of King Oedipus does not recognize the succession?

525–7   The leader of the Chorus can only refer to *familial* characteristics as an excuse, and is not prepared to recognize Antigone's arguments. Dramatically, it is important to try to head off a 'personal clash' too, and to give Creon time to compose his thoughts.

What do you think of Creon's reply (528–54)?

Figure 9   Still from first production of Jean Anouilh's *Antigone*, Théâtre de l'Atelier, February 1944, showing Antigone (Monelle Valentin) brought before Creon (Jean Davy). (Photo: Lipnitzki Viollet.)

In fact, his answer is not in any way statesmanlike or a response from the *state's* point of view to her argument: hence the need for Hegel to juxtapose lines 179–235 to Antigone's speech (see Introduction to set text, p.41). Creon is so angry that he gives everything away: he is revealed as a bully delighting in breaking down any opposition (527–33) and as a *weak man* unable to see anything in Antigone's speech other than a personal insult. The weakness is emphasized by his *failure to address Antigone face-to-face*: the third person 'she' shows that he is complaining to the Chorus about her as if she were not present (536–40). The gender-switch (541–2) reveals deeper fears, and is a kind of prefiguration of the end of the play. The bringing-in of Ismene (on no evidence) is almost para-noiac in a man meant to administer justice in the state (543–54). ◆

555–93 This dialogue gives us no new information, but serves to sow doubt in our minds about the loyalty of the Chorus (564–5), though we don't *know* if Antigone is right. The exchange of views about Eteocles and Polynices is not entirely clear in this translation, so please note that:

584 'Death' means the god Hades.

586–7 Means literally 'Who knows if those below (in this case Eteocles) will not see these things (i.e. the burial of Polynices) as right?' (Because, in the world below, he will not continue to bear hatred.)

588–9 Means that Eteocles *will* continue to hate his brother after death.

590–1 Means 'Even if they are joined in hate, I was born to join in loving my brothers (and therefore to join them together in love)'.

591–3 Important in stressing that Antigone's love is directed towards the dead more than the living – though these are Creon's words, they will be borne out when Haemon's love is insufficient/unable to prevent her death. He returns to the abhorrence of women ruling, acting beyond their 'gender-specific role'.

593–6 The Chorus, in the absence of stage directions in the Greek text, and with the actor wearing a mask, are needed to remind us *who* it is, and to describe her emotional state. Forget about the intimacy of television drama, and think of being in the back row of the theatre at Epidauros, before you dismiss these considerations.

597–655 The greatness of the dramatist is shown in the unexpectedness of Ismene's wish to share the guilt, and in Antigone (a great one for blood-relationships with her brothers) *rejecting* a similar act of 'joining in love' by her sister. You would expect Antigone to sort out truth from lying, but the idea that 'this is my work, not yours' (610) and that 'this is my death, not yours' (615–6) sounds like sisters squabbling over an apple. 'I gave myself to death' (630) is a pointer which confirms the opinions of those who see Antigone as abnormally in love with death, an idea which Creon can dimly appreciate.

641–8 Pay special attention to *the betrothal of Haemon* (more serious in that society than in ours). Haemon is contracted to the marriage and he will see Antigone as already his wife to whom and for whom he is responsible, especially as in this case she has no father or male blood-relations.

645 Haemon's grievances include his right 'to dispose of' the woman to whom he is betrothed. This is usurped by his father who brushes aside family custom here. See the note (p.398–9) about the possible attribution of this line to Antigone.

649 Another line variously attributed. In this translation the Chorus are shown beginning to have doubts about Creon's justice/tyranny.

651–5 Notice again the derogatory reference to expected female behaviour.

Lines 656–700: Second stasimon

leading to

Lines 701–4: Introduction of Haemon

The Chorus lament the ruin of a famous house/family (that of Oedipus) – sorrows which seem to be willed by the gods from one generation to the next. But in apparently blaming the gods, they blame Antigone and dare to glance at Creon (677–8). They refer to the law of Zeus (so often the god referred to in this play), but here again the reference is ambiguous and could refer to Oedipus' children or Creon (the fact that Creon is on stage is not important in this non-realistic part of the drama).

Lines 705–878: Third episode (2 actors and the leader)

709	Haemon, as *Creon's* son and *Antigone's* partner, shows conventional respect for his father and surprises us by his diplomacy.
715–22	Creon has views about the *oikos* as well as the *polis*. It is all rather like a feuding society when the stress is on enemies – 'to be paid back'.
723–30	The appeal to male bonding is followed by a rejection of the female – 'we don't want a bad woman in our *oikos*' – leading to a rejection of one woman, Antigone (730).
731–61	Here again we are surprised. This passage depends on Haemon's non-reaction to the first two paragraphs: Creon launches out into a general defence – state against rebellion, law against anarchy – that had rung true (possibly) at 179–235. But now it all seems so specious after what has intervened, and reads more like a spurious legalizing of his hatred for Antigone, confirmed by the lapse back into 'sexism' at 758–61, which is full of dramatic ironies.
735–6	Zeus in his aspect of guardian of the *oikos* (i.e. 'who defends all bonds of kindred blood' = *xunhaimon*). Puns upon Haemon/*haimon* = 'blood' are available in the Greek.
761–3	Again, the interposition of the leader averts a personal clash.
764–809	In any case, Haemon is clever and tries to win his father round. Notice how 781–2 quotes Creon's own words (229–30) and the argument about *bending* (797ff.) refers back to 526–35.
810–12	The speech seems to us to almost parody the non-committal attitude of a Greek Chorus, but serves to indicate a mid-point in the debate and perhaps in their changing attitude to Creon.
813–59	The shorter speech-lengths, one line each in the Greek, fit the transition to fierce argument and capping of the opponent's speeches. Notice that Creon's case is now that *she* is a rebel, and that there is no longer reference to Polynices.
843	Creon misunderstands and thinks that *he* is threatened. Haemon is already thinking that he *himself* will not survive Antigone (855–6).
860–78	Creon reverts to his cool resolve to put down Antigone; Ismene is superfluous and would complicate this plan. Of course, you can see 866–8 as a victory for the Chorus, but the Chorus do not *initiate* actions. Creon has already planned a cunning execution which will avoid the gods' revenge (873–4); but we had thought he did not believe in such inhibitions. Of course, actually killing somebody is rather different from a 'savage attack' on a *corpse*. Perhaps he is once again concerned with 'respect' – the thing must look right. Anyway, he is inconsistent: his original decree was for *stoning* (43), a sentence which would have been carried out by the whole community.

Lines 879–99: Third stasimon and reappearance of Antigone

879–94   The 'Love' hymned here is potentially destructive. But (891–2) in one respect its power is linked to laws, not in conflict with them. Presumably these are the unwritten primal divine laws which Antigone obeys.

895–9   The Chorus are now sufficiently moved (see 810–2) to contemplate changing sides.

Lines 900–1034: Fourth episode (2 actors, Leader and the Chorus)

In this section the actors and Chorus join in sung dialogue, known as *kommos* (for an explanation of the term, see Figure 4 above).

900–68   The tragic hero/ine is often allowed a chance, especially in Sophocles – either when sentence of death is pronounced, or when the tragic fall has taken place – to pour out those emotions which were held back in the earlier scenes. (Another example is Oedipus in *Oedipus the King*, after his blinding.) The drama is therefore at the furthest point from realism, and comments on 'Antigone breaking forth into self-pity' are inappropriate, since the art-form requires this emotional climax, regardless of the character so far established. (See further discussion at 4.5.2.) In any case it is doubtful whether the total consistency of character, which we expect today, exists in Classical drama, the Middle Ages, or even in Shakespeare (cf. Gertrude's speech on the death of Ophelia, which seems inconsistent with the character's previous utterances).

In the *kommos* most of the themes of the play are reiterated, but the inevitability of Death is emphasized: the Love/Death mood is now dominant in the parody of a wedding celebration hinted at in the first verse, though Creon (969–70) identifies what he hears as a dirge.

Read pp.45–50 of the Introduction to the set text and decide whether you think lines 995–1004 of the play should be deleted.

Discussion is included in the commentary.

978–1004   Antigone's last major speech rehearses the melancholy wish to join the 'growing family of the dead' (981), but progresses to make a point which some critics have found untenable (995–1004) and have even wished to delete, though its authenticity is as well established as any part of the text, since it is quoted by Aristotle in the next century in *Rhetoric*, 3.16.9. (On Aristotle's view, see Introduction to the set text, p.47.)

The point that Antigone makes was still commonplace in the late 'feudal' society of Albania in 1909:

> We sat round, while the Man-that-claimed-blood told his tale. His only son had wished to marry a certain widow, and gave her in token thereof a ring and £T.1. But her parents, whose property she was, would not recognize this betrothal, and sold her to another.
>
> 'My son', said the man, 'would have paid for her fully, and she wished to marry him. Then was he very angry, and would shoot her husband. But he bethought him, the husband was not guilty, for perhaps he knew not of her betrothal. The guilty ones were the men of her family who sold her. To clear his honour, he shot one of her brothers. Then another brother shot my son, and I have no other. I want blood for my son's blood. They are to blame. They first put shame on him, and then killed him.'

The old man thought long over the case, and asked questions. Then he said one was dead on either side, and it were better the blood were laid. He advised a sitting of Elders (a *medjliss*) to compound the feud – which was also the Padre's advice. All who heard agreed with the old man, save him who heard the cry of his son's blood, and he would hearken to nothing else.

What was the woman's point of view? In these tales, she has neither voice nor choice – *adet* (custom) passes over her like a Juggernaut car.

To judge by a twentieth-century and West European standard the feelings of a people in such a primitive state of human development would be foolish. It is perhaps equally foolish to attempt to analyse them at all. Here, as in Montenegro, women tell you frankly that, of course, a woman loves her brother better than her husband. She can have another husband and another child, but a brother can never be replaced. Her brother is of her own blood – her own tribe.

(Edith Durham, High Albania, Virago 1985, pp.90–1.)

Further, one must remember that the 'crime' which had produced Antigone and her siblings – Oedipus' marriage with his mother – is so well-known to the audience as not to need mentioning. This 'kind' of brother is unique. Antigone makes it clear that the play is not only about 'Hades' burial-rite' versus 'state is law' but about claims of kin (*oikos*) versus claims of state (*polis*). It is not the burial, but the brotherhood, which spurred her on to action. The fact that she challenges Creon not for a *general* principle but a *particular* relationship may seem to some less 'noble', but it fills out the *humanity* of what might have been an abstract and *inhuman* character. This speech seems to me to make Antigone understandable – we may all admire a principle, but it needs a personal stimulus to act. (Examples come to mind of mothers of 'the disappeared' in Argentina, or villagers in Britain campaigning against nuclear dumping, but these may seem out of date by the time you read this.)

1005– **1021**	The speech now swells out to embrace archetypal tragic situations and religious questions.
	a) 'I descend alive to the caverns of the dead' (1012), i.e. the facing of death by the sacrificial victim/scapegoat.
1025	It may be that the moment of realization forces Antigone to cry out: but this would be in the tradition of this drama, rather than psychological realism. Perhaps she (and the audience) had expected the people to revolt or the Chorus to intervene, or even the gods to materialize – as they do in many Greek plays at a point like this.
1031	I suppose one could suggest that this is an appeal for intervention: she emphasizes (ignoring Ismene) that she is the last of the children of the royal house and may have thought all along that she commanded more loyalty from the people than Creon. More simply, the last speech shows her affirming her nobility, and calling out for all (including the audience who are drawn into the action) to bear witness.

Lines 1035–90: Fourth stasimon

Antigone and others having found no parallel, the Chorus produce the case of Danae and less well-known parallels. In each case the point is the finality of such premature entombments: no hope of recovery is dwelt upon, though Danae, for example, became the bride of Zeus in her 'brazen' prison.

Lines 1090–1238: Fifth episode (2 actors and the Leader)

1090   Tiresias is probably best known from *Oedipus the King* – a later play by Sophocles. This exchange reads like a first go at a much more complex confrontation in the later play. Gods do not appear in these plays, but Tiresias, who *knows* the will of the gods, is a kind of *deus ex machina* (literally a 'god out of a machine' who was let down onto the stage by the crane at a critical moment when the human beings had created an insoluble problem), a device used in other plays to unravel the knot of the action.

1124   The pollution of the altars is similar to the pollution of Thebes in *Oedipus the King*. So is the accusation that Tiresias is bribed by dissidents (1161).

1218–38   Creon's collapse and repentance is spectacular, but easy to prophesy from the weaknesses already apparent in his character. Now that he understands that Haemon is in danger, he is 'turned round'. The interest of the ending of the play is heightened by having the 'tyrant' now acting to free his victim.

Lines 1238–72: Hyporcheme – a dance-song of joy

The Chorus, and we ourselves, are temporarily elated. Hope is still possible; perhaps we are witnessing a tragi-comedy like certain plays of Euripides, in which 'catastrophe is averted'.

1239   Dionysos is appropriately honoured at his festival too. This song is certainly to be accompanied by dancing.

Lines 1272–1470: Exodos (3 actors and Leader)

1272–84   The messenger (needed to relate events off-stage) can weaken tension by delay. We begin with the basic point of all tragedy, as the Greeks and medievals saw it – the fall from high estate. Notice how this is blamed on *Fortune*: there is no moral suggestion at this stage.

1285–99   At first the simple facts are narrated, and Tiresias' prophecy is confirmed.

1300   Eurydice, a new character, introduced as late as this to show 'reaction' to the news, is again interesting as a 'trial run' for Jocasta in *Oedipus the King*.

1317–71   The messenger declaims the 'epic narrative' of events in a conventional long speech. This is a 'set piece.' One may assume that the narrative (and its language) were sufficient then to hold the audience: the Greeks delighted in long speeches, which they encountered in real life in the law-courts and in political debate (see Thucydides). Nowadays action, mime, and interruption are needed to get through anything as long as this in most productions of Shakespeare.

1336   Notice how direct quotation of Creon's words is used to create 'a play within a speech'.

1347   Though Antigone's death is described, there is no word of sorrow for *this* death from Creon now or later. Nor does he regret the insult to Polynices.

1372–3   The little moral is unexpectedly trite, but serves to indicate the end of the narrative.

1387–8   Though death is off-stage, the visible evidence is brought to the attention of the audience.

1388–1470   The release of emotion is indicated by the shorter lyric lines and the dialogue with the Chorus (*kommos*). Compare *Prometheus Bound*.

1419   A fairly common piece of staging (*ekkuklema*) is used to expose the bodies from within the palace (cf. Aeschylus' *Agamemnon*). Perhaps the same device is used in reverse at the end of *Prometheus Bound*.

1428   The audience would have known that one of Creon's sons had already died in the battle or, according to Euripides, had sacrificed himself to Ares in order to ensure the Thebans' success.

1458   There is no hope. (Here we could comment on the difference between this and tragedy written in the Christian era, even by those who have abandoned Christianity. There is *hope* at the end of *King Lear*, often thought of as an extreme example of a 'godless play'.)

1459–65 Even to the end he sees himself the victim of an error of judgement, of a kind of trap which he has sprung unconsciously, and it is interesting that no mention is made of Antigone by name.

Why?

Discussion _____

To preserve our sympathy for Creon in his tragedy. Any mention of Antigone – who has had her lament – would switch our attention back to her. Nevertheless, it is worth noting that no judgement is passed on:

a)   whether the unwritten laws were right;

b)   whether Zeus and Hades really intervened, though Tiresias had explained that they were affronted. Perhaps it is a 'purely human' tragedy in which the gods played no part. ◆

1466–70 The final Chorus, however, takes up Antigone's last words, 'reverence for the gods', and so knits the play together (although this is not true of the words in the Greek text). Notice the distancing effect of these lines, as if the action were already 'over there' and fading away.

4.5   General essays

These pick up points made at 4.3.1 and go over some of the questions you were asked to keep in mind while reading the play.

4.5.1   Sophocles and the gods

Go quickly through the text and note down some of the major references to the gods. (Note that Death = Hades, both an underworld god and a location.) Then think back to Prometheus Bound. *What major difference is there between 'the gods' in the two plays? Do you think Sophocles believes in 'the gods' in the same way as Aeschylus? Even if you think that, in this play, Sophocles is careful not to commit himself to the literal existence of 'the gods', does the play still make sense as a play about human beings?*

Discussion _____

The major difference is of course that in *Prometheus Bound* the gods actually appear on stage or, as in the case of Zeus, take a clearly-defined part in the action of the play, even if they don't appear. Aeschylus' treatment of the gods owes a good deal to Homer, Hesiod and the mythological material which Aeschylus is using. Aeschylus' own personal beliefs are not accessible to us, except by inference from the plays, and it might be easier to say that his audience presumably accepted the physical appearance of the gods without bursting into laughter. (With Euripides, who occasionally introduces the gods *ex machina* to tidy up insoluble problems, it is impossible to know how the audience reacted, and Euripides has, from time to time, been represented as a 'comedian' or as an early Ibsen/Shaw figure engaged in mocking established beliefs. You can think about this when you read *The Women of Troy* in Block 4 and *The Bacchae* in Block 5. In Aristophanes' comedies, when gods and heroes appear in person, the effect is ludicrous.) Sophocles avoids this by locating the drama (i.e. the characters in action) indisputably in the human sphere, and this is why *Antigone* still 'makes sense'. In fact, it is not at all clear *what* the gods *think* about Antigone and Creon; we are told by human beings – and Tiresias is very important here – what the gods are supposed to be thinking, but even Tiresias could be taken as a man with a grudge who knows how to put the frighteners on.

Each 'god' can therefore be taken as a summary formulation of particular human desires/fears, though I must make it clear that such rationalist or 'advanced thinking' is not typical of the Greeks. To Creon, Zeus approves of order in the state: to Antigone, Hades (or Zeus Chthonios, the god of funeral rights/rites) approves of her action. A twentieth-century audience would have no difficulty in substituting a psychological 'inner' voice for these deities, and we might argue that Antigone, in her last speeches, does break down, when she thinks that 'the gods' have deserted her (lines 1013–34). It is extremely unlikely that a Greek audience would have seen things in this way, and Sophocles may have seemed to them to have preserved respect for the gods by keeping them off-stage.   ◆

What, then, are we to make of the invocation of the gods and associated 'messages' from them in songs by the Chorus? In what sense do we take the Ode to Man (376– 416) or the Song to Dionysos (1238–73) for example?

Discussion _____

You might argue that the Chorus is some kind of archaic survival (from the *dithyramb*, a song in honour of Dionysos) and that clever though Sophocles is at 'using the Chorus as a character', the audience still expected the Chorus to bear a religious/'Three Choirs Festival' role in the Dionysos Festival at Athens and to sing appropriate hymns. So, it might be said, the Song to Dionysos is detachable from the play (when Sophocles, aged 90, was defending himself against the accusation that he was senile and unable to manage his estate, he quoted a 'detached ode' from *Oedipus at Colonus*) – and the same description might apply to the Ode to Man. On the other hand, the Chorus is often described as 'mediating between the action of the play and the audience': it occupied this physical position in the *orchestra* of the Greek stage and it is often seen as a normalizing voice, chastening the extremes of emotion voiced by the actors, and bringing out equivocal propositions – such as 'Call no man happy until he is dead' (*Oedipus the King*) – which are sometimes, though not in the major plays of Aeschylus and Sophocles, quite fatuously inappropriate.   ◆

Another point of view is that the specifically religious hymns/songs do contain divine messages or helpful analogies from religion/mythology which are 'what a god might have said had one been present'. So:

1   The Ode to Man praises his ingenuity, but points out that he has not been able to find a way round Death – concealing a message to Creon as well as, possibly, reflecting on the ingenuity of the unknown 'burier' of Polynices.

2   The Hymn to Eros warns us that love is a more powerful force than reason and that people (like Creon) who underestimate it are in for a surprise.

3   The Hymn to Dionysos, usually taken as an expression of hope from the Chorus that all the impending misfortune will be reversed by the 'national god of Thebes' (Dionysos being the equivalent of Athene at Athens), must surely have made the audience shudder with remembrance of the legend of Pentheus and how Dionysos actually *did* come to Thebes, destroying all opposition (you will be studying a tragedy based on this theme in Block 5). Creon, like Pentheus, has failed to take account of the 'dark gods', the

irrational forces which subsume the daylight world of family and state: his family is destroyed, and his proud boasting of kingship reduced to almost infantile behaviour. His role in both *polis* and *oikos* is annihilated.

In all three cases you could imagine a modern production with special lighting or visual effects in which Hades/Death, Eros and Dionysos actually appeared/materialized for a brief moment during these choruses – even in Sophocles' production, the dance of which we have no record could have mimed the power of these deities.

All this is 'might' and 'could'. Perhaps it is easier to stick to the text and say that the Chorus pray to gods to intervene, and we may or may not see the subsequent events of the play as the results of these prayers, because everything can still be accounted for on a purely human level. Such 'inconsistency' was typical of the Greeks' perception of the role of the gods in ordinary life, too.

4.5.2 Sophocles and the human characters

What do you see as the Sophoclean way of representing human beings – 'common' to Antigone and Creon, for example? Think of the commonly accepted theory of tragedy, that the hero/heroine falls because of an error or 'tragic flaw'. What is Sophoclean tragedy? What makes his people (is it right to call them 'people'?) behave in one way rather than another? Are the characters, once established, consistent in their behaviour?

Discussion _____

These are all big questions, and you could well want to duck them, or request an exit to the side of the course through which it might be possible to quickly read a lot of Greek and other tragedy and then return refreshed and able to deal with the subject under discussion. And a number of much bigger issues lurk in the thickets – how do we recognize *character* from a few words and stage conventions, so that we know most of what we need to know about Antigone after the first scene with Ismene. Characters help to define each other, as it were. Creon is more difficult to interpret than anybody else, it would seem, depending on whether, like Hegel, you take his speeches at face-value, or whether, as in the notes I supplied in the commentary, you receive the immediate impression that he is 'the tyrant' who speaks with double tongue, praising the state while he is in fact looking for somebody to bully. Or perhaps he changes character from 'statesman' to 'tyrant' during the course of the play.

Sophoclean tragedy, to hazard a generalization, seems to be self-generated. Creon makes mistakes which bring retribution; this is very Greek: perhaps 'misjudgements' is a better phrase than 'mistakes', because the ruler *judges* in all senses – both situations and people. He resembles other Sophoclean males – bull-like figures, Oedipus the King and Ajax, who fall into the net or trap, devised partly by themselves though 'the gods' are always invoked. They are then goaded like the bull, and reduced to an animal-like state: Oedipus screams in his self-inflicted blindness, Ajax goes mad and is covered in the blood of butchered animals, and Creon is similarly reduced to tears and groans. In each case, can we apply the dictum of Aristotle, that it is the good man falling from power who is the most 'tragic'? Perhaps not to Creon, and in any case, you will say, the play is called *Antigone*, and it should not be called that if she is simply the victim and then the instrument of Creon's fall.

In what, then, does the tragedy of Antigone consist? Is she a totally virtuous person, unjustly condemned? In which case her blood cries out for vengeance and is avenged by 'the gods': but is this tragedy? Or is it that she has a fault, and that this fault is related to that of Creon and the other figures mentioned above? In which case you would need to prove that she is not faultless. Consider this point of view: Antigone is not wholly noble, she is equally a victim of overwhelming/over-reaching pride ('stubbornness') as is Creon – pride in her isolated righteousness. (See Introduction to *Antigone*, p.51.) She is like the other Sophoclean figures in that she pushes one idea too far. Oedipus must find out the truth, Ajax feels that he has been slighted and cannot retreat from the state of paranoia into which he is led by this assumption. So Antigone is not going to compromise, and, like Prometheus, she is responsible for what happens to her because she knows that she is *provoking* the ruler to punish her.

Most people will not accept this interpretation, and for them Antigone is blameless. We shall need to return to this point later, but it may seem to leave us with an inadequate account of the play. The Chorus several times comment 'like father, like daughter', and the curse on the house of Oedipus is left as the only remaining 'explanation' of her plight, throwing the cause of the tragedy back from Antigone to 'the gods'.

With regard to the third and fourth questions, we must understand that we are not reading about *characters* in a nineteenth-century novel or engaging in a psychoanalytic study of the depths of the mind. (Remember the problems of *tone* in the exchanges between Prometheus and Oceanus?) Greek tragedy is public performance, and the masks inevitably lead to simplification: this was easier to see in *Prometheus Bound* where, on the whole, the characters are totally consistent: Prometheus suffers, but continues defiant; Io is a goaded victim, and so on. With Sophocles we have moved on. Creon is not just 'the ruler', any old ruler, he is particularized; Antigone and Ismene are more than just the strong and the weak sister. All of these act *unexpectedly* at times, as do Haemon and, we suppose, Eurydice.

But is this simply to be explained as 'inconsistency of characters'? The fact that Ismene changes sides, that Antigone perhaps begins to break down in the face of death, that even Creon, I think, demands our sympathy at the end of the play, is not because characters are inconsistent, but because they are human – and being human, they will crack under strain, or are, like the interesting Ismene, full of surprises. Certainly it is worth considering the idea that Sophoclean tragedy shows normal human beings being tested in extreme situations which are conceivable within human experience, in contrast with Aeschylus (in *Agamemnon*) showing extraordinary human beings (Klytemnestra or Cassandra) or beings of god-like proportions (in *Prometheus Bound*) in situations beyond normal human experience. There is a sense in which we have all met people like Antigone and Ismene, whereas we are unlikely to have encountered a Prometheus.   ◆

4.5.3   Gender in *Antigone*

Is there a case for regarding Antigone *as a play about male and female roles in society? Does Antigone, unlike Ismene, for example, fail to act submissively as a woman should? What is Creon's reaction? How would the audience, which may have included women, have 'received' this?*

Discussion _____

You may feel, at first, that this is an example of feminist ideas being applied to an ancient text which cannot respond to them, and that it is wrong to expect women from the past to behave according to standards of the 1990s. I would argue, that, even without feminism to guide us, it would be odd if we did not notice:

a)   the constant reference by Creon to the fact that his maleness is challenged – for example, the long speech to Haemon (lines 712–61, especially the ending), and see the Introduction, p.43;

b)   the idea, expressed by her opponents, that Antigone is mad, temporarily unhinged by passion, temporarily acting like her father (for example, 525–7), that in fact she is going beyond the *normal* limit of female behaviour. This is all there in the opening dialogue with Ismene (for example, 74–5):

> Remember we are women,
> we're not born to contend with men.

We have anecdotal evidence that the play *Antigone* was so popular that Sophocles was given public office: his high reputation among his contemporaries needs to be considered again and again in discussing this and similar questions. When you consider the role assigned to women in fifth-century Athens (see *WA* passim, especially 4.23–31), it seems remarkable that in a city where women had *no* public life, such a challenging play with a woman as the major character won the prize, and was not shouted down as subversive. ♦

Historical note of caution

Note, though, that Greek plays are usually set in the mythological pre-history of Greece, in the time of Homer and Herakles. Women have powerful roles – for example, Klytemnestra, Medea, Hecuba, Cassandra, Elektra – throughout 'the world of Greek drama', and the audience may have accepted:

1 *that times were once different* and that women – for example, the Amazons – did once rule and had more power. Note that it is comic when Aristophanes, in *Lysistrata* for example, shows them trying to take power in the Athenian state.

2 *that art is different from life*, and that the drama was a vehicle for 'displaying' emotions usually held back or suppressed: and that therefore women in the audience would applaud Antigone all the more for her defiance, knowing full well that they would never dare do likewise. Like Nora in Ibsen's *A Doll's House*, who walks out of the marital home, she does what was inconceivable for most women in real life.

4.5.4   Symbolism and poetic drama

I now want to shift the discussion on to a different plane. In the first place, I would like you to think about the nature of the text in front of us. It is a play in verse, and not a prose documentary about an incident in the Theban Civil War. If you consider the play *as a poem*, a new area of discussion is open to us, which we normally call the *sub-text*.

In former times Sophocles was often thought of as simple and straightforward, a truly classical writer. Aeschylus on the other hand was given to astounding flights of 'poetry', and in the work of Euripides, whom we have yet to meet, complex patterns of symbolism either support or contradict the official action of the drama.

In *Antigone* there is a fairly simple pattern of associations which should be noted, though Sophocles does not use imagery in the way that Shakespeare does, for example, except in the choruses.

In his speeches, what comparisons does Creon make to ideas of control? Bring in the 'Ode to Man' chorus or other characters' speeches if you wish, to show how the images are developed.

Discussion _____

Creon guides and *controls the ship* of state (line 180) and Man also holds his course on a ship (381). Creon keeps the city on course (1097 and 1282). He refers to the *taming or management of horses* as a picture of his managerial skills (331–2), and again this is developed by the Chorus (393–4). In answer to Antigone's attack, he refers again to the taming of horses (532–3). ♦

Look again at the 'Ode to Man' (376–416). What other pictures are there of Man's activities and how do they relate to the two already mentioned as qualities of Creon?

Discussion _____

Man *plows* with the aid of his horses, so wearing away the Earth (382–5), and he *snares* wild creatures, birds, beasts and fish (386–90). He *rules the city* with his law, and *shelters from the arrows* and *shafts* of the weather (395–400). All this culminates in the picture of an ideal city (409–12) from which undesirables are to be ejected. The idea of control is developed into *containment*.

A large amount of this imagery can be applied simply to Creon and his actions, and also to his city. Thebes is famous for its seven gates (118), but gates delimit a controlled area, as do those of the palace (23): the punishment for burying Polynices is to be stoned *within the city walls* (42); the temples of Thebes are 'ringed' with pillars' (323). Antigone tells Creon that its citizens 'keep their tongues *in leash*' (570); he has no time for people who '*step out of line*' (746). Antigone is captured by the sentries who behave 'like *hunters*' (481); Antigone and Ismene are tied up on Creon's orders – 'no more *running loose*' (653). Finally, Creon defies storms of *spears* (744) and *arrows* (1145 and 1206).

You may feel that many of these examples are clichés in English and probably in Greek too, but one of the functions of the poet is to make old clichés live and to bring out their meaning. Putting all this together, we arrive at a Creon whose attempts to *contain* everything are paralleled by the achievements of Man who attempts to contain the world of Nature. ◆

How does that world of nature respond? Look for examples of imagery opposed to that listed above. N.B. It will not only be negative. Who is brought into prominence by the opposed symbols?

Discussion _____

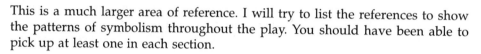

This is a much larger area of reference. I will try to list the references to show the patterns of symbolism throughout the play. You should have been able to pick up at least one in each section.

Firstly, the danger to ships from the power of the storm. Look at the whole of the Chorus beginning at line 656. The 'uncontrolled' imagery in the first part is opposed to the first image in the Ode to Man. The storm gathers its power, leads towards ruin, and 'our high hopes' (690) are a 'delusion' (692). Haemon tells Creon that the way to survive while sailing a ship is to go with the wind, not to defy it (800–803). Ships cannot save us, nor the 'towered walls' of cities, from the power of fate (1045–50).

Secondly, there are many references to untamed creatures who live in the *wild*. Birds and dogs are mentioned because of their literal existence as devourers of Polynices' corpse, but they also have a free existence – 'the wild dogs and wheeling vultures' (781), 'birds that scan the field and feast to their heart's content' (36). In one of the few 'Shakespearian images', Antigone is compared to:

> a bird come back to an empty nest,
> peering into its bed, and all the babies gone ...
>
> (472–3)

Thirdly, you could look positively at the symbols of the storm, the wind, the wild places and their associations. Besides the Chorus mentioned above, look at the apostrophe to love (879ff.) – love 'ranges the seas', is out in the shepherds' huts 'in the wilds'. Look also at the Hymn to Dionysos (1239ff.) – the son of thunder (1241), who appears on mountains, shores and wild places (1240–64) *outside the city*. To Creon these forces are Anarchy (751), and will destroy cities and houses (753). But we know from the Chorus that they are the symbols of the gods and their power.

In fact, these references help us to see that there is a whole *uncontained* 'third realm' outside both *polis* and *oikos*, which is opposed to both of them. The various stages in the story of Antigone show her to be, perhaps unconsciously, in tune with this realm and, at a later stage, entering into it. This helps to give stature and power to her cause.

Right at the beginning she pulls Ismene 'out here, past the gates' (22–3): her burial of Polynices is mysteriously accomplished by the assistance of a whirlwind (463ff.). She is literally sent by Creon 'down some wild, desolate path' (870) and walled up in a cave ('vault'), and these ideas of desert and cave are reiterated until they become symbols firmly associated with Antigone. Cave and grave, womb and tomb are pulled into one *'bridal vault where all are laid to rest'* (899) and the permutations of this image are explored in her succeeding dialogue with the Chorus (900–42). ◆

Please read these lines again now.

Like Niobe she will be isolated and yet become at one with Nature: notice that even her references to her own city are not to its towers and walls (Creon's symbols) but to the springs of the river and the trees of the holy grove (935–6).

So Antigone 'descends alive to the *caverns* of the dead' (1012) still agitated by 'rough *winds*' of passion (1022). The next chorus explores further examples of the bridal-vault, and reflects that 'caverns' (1084) and 'gales' (1086) were unable to save Cleopatra, daughter of the North Wind, from Death (the legend is obscure, see the note on pp.402–3 of the set text).

In Tiresias' speech we learn that the birds are behaving strangely, and they pollute the altars, bringing the carrion *from* the wild *into* the city. I realize that Tiresias is literally an augur, who studies the behaviour of birds, and that the birds literally tear the corpse of Polynices, but it is *the invasion of the city by the wild* that points up the symbolic background. The birds are, as it were, 'trying to tell us something'.

Similarly, while Eurydice tells us that she was literally 'opening the doors' (1306) – and the Greek word for 'doors' is *pulai*, the same as the word translated as 'gates' at lines 22–3 – she is trying to get out into the air, to establish contact between the *oikos* of Creon and the gods, to *open the oikos* to a message from outside. It is too late. The messenger brings the news of Antigone's suicide and Haemon's death in the hollow cave, a 'wedding chamber' where the parody of a marriage is enacted (1328–71).

It is in parallel to this repetition of the *bridal vault*, that Creon repeats the gist of line 870. Now it is he who has 'gone down the darkest road' (1336–7) and has been driven 'down that *wild savage path*' (1404) out of the enclosed city and towards the new experience provided by the wild desert, which finally destroys him.

4.5.5 Different readings of *Antigone*

Read through the Introduction to the set book again, concentrating especially on the Hegel interpretation, p.41, and noting the editor's (Knox's) rather 'revisionist' conclusions (pp.52–3) that because 'the gods do not praise Antigone, nor does anyone else in the play' (except Haemon, and he is in love), therefore the play is not a clearcut vindication of Antigone's position. What do you think the play's message is? How does its dramatic structure reinforce that message? (At this point, replay the Interactive Cassette, Cassette 1, Band 3.)

INTERACTIVE

Discussion

It seems difficult to believe that a play which was as 'unclear' as Knox seems to find it would have been so praised. I cannot tell what you have made of it, but you have been introduced to Hegel's position, which is that the play is poised between two balanced rights – those of the state and the citizen. Hegel's reading is based largely upon lines 179–235 being taken at face value, and contrasted with lines 499–524: the right of the state to demand obedience to its laws from its citizens, and the right of the individual to oppose her conscience to those laws. He says of Creon and Antigone: 'In the view of the Eternal Justice, both were wrong, because they were one-sided, but at the same time both were right.' The modern versions that are discussed in the Introduction are not so 'half-hearted' – 'the natural instinct of all modern readers and playgoers is to sympathize fully with Antigone, the rebel and martyr' (Introduction, p.38).

Such readings or versions simplify the play too much: and they don't make it clear how to incorporate the second part of the play into 'the message', since Antigone leaves the stage at line 1034 and our interest must be continued. Sophoclean drama has an unusual way of going beyond the point where a modern dramatist would put the final curtain. The play's structure is like that of a wave – the forces against Antigone wash *up* to the high point, Antigone's last speech as she goes to death: in the remainder of the play the wave washes *back*, as it were, and takes Creon's family with it. 'The gods' are provoked: 'the gods' respond. Read again the last chorus (lines 1486–70) – there is no escape from the gods' final and *massive* reaction to human pride. As I have pointed out, even with no 'gods', the play still works as an example of psychological 'inner' forces exacting their retribution. ♦

Sir Richard Jebb, the most famous nineteenth-century editor of the play, had none of Knox's doubt or vagueness. To him the play was crystal-clear:

> The simplicity of the plot is due to the clearness with which two principles are opposed to each other.

> (Introduction to Cambridge Abridged Edition, p.xviii)

(He means 'the State's laws' and 'the private conscience.') Jebb concludes his discussion:

> Sophocles has allowed Creon to put his case ably, and (in a measure from which an inferior artist might have shrunk) he has been content to make Antigone merely a nobly heroic woman, not a being exempt from human passion and human weakness; but none the less does he mean us to feel that, in this controversy, the right is wholly with her, and the wrong wholly with her judge.

> (ibid., p.xix)

These are strong and confident words, spoken from the heart of the Victorian 'liberal' ideology, for which we must make certain allowances. Nevertheless, they seem to me nearer than Knox ever gets to explaining why this play has held the attention of the world for so long.

4.6 Further Reading on *Antigone*

4.6.1 Other translations or versions

If you have time, read the translation by Tom Paulin, *The Riot Act* (London, Faber, 1985), in which the history of Northern Ireland is a back-cloth to the play. You may be surprised by some of the text. For example, the Choric Ode to Man (lines 377–416) is reduced to three five-line stanzas of ironical comment on humanity's so-called 'scientific achievements'.

The version by Anouilh is still available in English:

ANOUILH, J. (1960) *Antigone*, London, Methuen.

Brecht used Hölderlin's nineteenth-century translation, which is still played in Germany. He left us a valuable introduction to his 1948 production, available in *Brecht on Theatre*, translated by John Willett (New York, Hill and Wang, 1964). See pp.209–215, 'Masterful treatment of a model'.

4.6.2 The *Antigone* in Western literature

See George Steiner, *Antigones* (Oxford, Oxford University Press, 1984) for a full account of the history of the play. *Antigone* – like *Faust, Don Juan*, or *Hamlet* – has become one of the most regularly performed plays in the European theatre, particularly since Hegel. The figure of Antigone is also an easily recognizable point of literary reference, besides being a moral ideal. Steiner explains that the play has undergone many *adaptations* rather than translations and suggests that these re-writings are a form of criticism of the text, as well as clearly illustrating various stages in the interpretation of the play. The adaptations indicate by their very omissions what producers see as intractable material, while the extended version of some scenes show what is to be stressed. See in particular, Athol Fugard, 'The Island', in *Statements* (Oxford, Oxford University Press, 1974). Fugard dramatizes the effect that preparing a performance of the *Antigone* had on political prisoners on Robben Island. President Nelson Mandela of South Africa refers in his memoirs to just such an occasion, commenting on the impact of Antigone's situation: 'She was in her own way a freedom fighter, for she defied the law on the ground that it was unjust.' Furthermore, he describes how playing the role of Creon enabled him to confront, in prospect, the responsibilities of power: '[Creon's] inflexibility and blindness ill become a leader, for a leader must temper justice with mercy' (N. Mandela, *Long Walk to Freedom*, Abacus, 1995, p.541).

4.6.3 Criticism etc.

In addition to the Select Bibliography of Sophocles provided on pp.421–3 of the set book, please note the following books:

TAPLIN, O. (1977) *The Stagecraft of Aeschylus*, Oxford, Oxford University Press; while obviously not about Sophocles, this has a good appendix on 'The stage resources of fifth-century theatre' (also mentioned in 2.8.2 in the context of *Prometheus Bound*).

GOLDHILL, S. (1986) *Reading Greek Tragedy*, Cambridge, Cambridge University Press. Goldhill discusses the *Antigone* in his chapter on 'Relations and relationships', pp.88–106. I particularly urge you to take to heart his final remarks (p.286):

> It is because tragedy is not reducible to a simple 'message', because these dramas are not played out or exhausted in a single reading or performance, that readers return again and again to ancient tragedy. The continuing response to Greek tragedy is not simply each generation, each reader, or each reader at different times, reaching towards some eternally fixed beauty or immutable truth encapsulated in the glory that was Greek tragedy, but being faced with the problems, tensions and uncertainities that these texts involve. It is in reading and responding to the continually unsettling and challenging questions set in motion by these plays that Greek tragedy is performed and experienced.

5   OEDIPUS THE KING

5.1   Introduction

In your Sophocles set book for the course, *Antigone*, *Oedipus the King* and *Oedipus at Colonus* are translated as 'The Three Theban Plays'. Together they relate the story of Oedipus and his family up to his death and beyond: the ending is the story you have just read in *Antigone* – the culmination of the curse on the house of Labdacus (Oedipus' grandfather).

The three plays are sometimes described as 'The Theban Trilogy', but this is a modern, popular misnomer: despite the fact that in modern performance they are often taken as a sequence, the plays were composed individually – at widely different stages of Sophocles' career. *Antigone* was the earliest (441 BCE); *Oedipus The King* (the earliest part of the story) was written *c*.430 (date not certain); and *Oedipus at Colonus* was presented in 401 BCE, several years after Sophocles' death. I give this information simply to warn against the assumption that there is *close* cross-reference of themes, character etc. between the plays. This is not to say, however, that no comparisons are possible!

Before you read *Oedipus The King*, I suggest you look back briefly at the outline of the play given in Section 4.2 above and the glimpses of the story in *Antigone* (lines 1–8, 60–66, 950–54). You might also like to read Bernard Knox's introduction to *Oedipus The King* in the Penguin, pp.131–53 (though note that this tends to emphasize a single aspect of the play, which I deal with under 'Oedipus, tragic mistakes and the gods'; see also Knox in the bibliography).

Then read the play straight through (referring to Knox's notes as necessary: Penguin translation, pp.405–13). I have not given you a list of topics because, in my experience, a concentrated read – as far as possible in one session – is the best initial approach to *Oedipus The King*.

Then return to this block. (Note that I shall not dwell on those aspects – for example, the use of three actors – that have been discussed fully in Section 4. Most of the important aspects of staging etc. discussed in Section 4 can be applied to *Oedipus The King*.)

5.2 The story and Sophocles' treatment

As with many other tragedies, the story had been dramatized before (for example by Aeschylus), and the events are briefly narrated as far back as Homer, *Odyssey* 11, 271ff. Sophocles is choosing his own particular treatment of the tradition.

Let's start with an aspect that strikes many initial readers, and may well have struck you – the contrast between Oedipus the highly intelligent man who guessed the Sphinx's riddle (44ff.), and shows a continuous desire to find out what has happened (301ff.), and Oedipus who fails to realize the truth despite being told it directly as early as 401 by Tiresias. Why do you think Sophocles violated everyday probability in this way?

Discussion _____

There are a number of possible answers:

1   Tragedy is not 'everyday' but a highly non-naturalistic medium; Sophocles was intent on creating suspense. Everybody would have known the story beforehand (as you may well have done). What is important is not Oedipus the detective in a 'whodunit' à la Agatha Christie, where the identity of the murderer is the main point, but an exploration of the way in which Oedipus and others react to the situation – a 'psychological thriller' (more like P.D. James?).

2   Making Oedipus 'slow' about guessing the truth of his birth allows the audience to experience the full horror – in slow motion, as it were – because, of course, they know the truth long before Oedipus and can experience sympathetic emotion at all his wrong inferences and increasing desperation.

3   The slow pace allows the development of a major thematic contrast between truth and appearance: Oedipus the knowledgeable and Oedipus totally ignorant of his real identity; Oedipus the saviour and benefactor of Thebes and Oedipus in reality polluted by two crimes regarded with instinctive horror – parricide and incest; Oedipus the solver of the riddle

of the Sphinx and Oedipus who cannot solve the riddle of his own existence. The more he exercises intelligence and seeks truth, the more he creates
his own destruction. ♦

The opposition between truth and appearance is continually revealed to the
audience by statements of Oedipus that have two levels of meaning, an innocent surface and an underlying significance that reveals the truth to the audience in dramatic irony. Consider, for example, lines 71–3 ('Well I know ... not
one is sick as I') where 'sick' refers not only to Oedipus' concern for the citizens
of Thebes, but to his own inner pollution (the word for 'sick' is repeated three
times in the Greek, as in the translation). Consider, too, line 156 where Oedipus'
assurance that he will act 'not to assist some distant kinsman' turns out to be
only too true when the 'kinsman' is revealed to be his own father (see also
248–9, 285, 301). More complex ambiguity occurs – for example, in 296ff. –
where the innocent 'blood-bond' between Oedipus, Laius and Jocasta
(Oedipus' surface meaning) can also be taken to refer to the incest (see the note
on p.407). These ironies are for the audience to appreciate – the close relation
between seeming and truth.

The irony is encapsulated in Oedipus' name, in two ways. Firstly the name is
similar to the Greek for 'swollen foot' – betraying the piercing of Oedipus' feet
as a baby. (Note that in the translation, the modern stage directions for the first
scene refer to a 'tell-tale limp'; textual warrant for this is lines 1131–5, by which
point the story is unravelling!) The Greeks were partial to puns of this kind, and
believed that they contained hidden truth; in this case the name is the clue to
Oedipus' identity, which is there for all to see.

Secondly, his name is closely linked in sound to the Greek *oida*, which means 'I
know'; so here is a second irony, the ignorant Oedipus (the Greek spells it
*Oidi*pous) has a name which suggests knowledge (see also line 54, and the note
on p.406). In 451 Oedipus, in furious altercation with Tiresias, ironically calls
himself 'Oedipus the ignorant', inadvertently speaking the truth.

This knowledge/appearance polarity is also closely related to light/darkness.
Oedipus, in wishing to cast light on the pollution that has caused the Theban
plague, plunges further into the darkness of his own identity (which 'blind'
Tiresias tells him about, 512ff.). The final discovery of the truth, the light of his
own identity, causes him to put himself into perpetual darkness by blinding
himself. Oedipus the all-seeing (150ff.) is really blind; only when he really sees
(1306 ff.) does he deprive himself of sight.

On one level, then, the artificiality of the plot of *Oedipus The King* represents the
articulation of the above polarities; the 'terror of coincidence' covers both events
outside the action of the play (survival of baby Oedipus, his murder of Laius,
his arrival in Thebes and marriage to Jocasta) and events within the drama (the
arrival of the Corinthian messenger, who is also the shepherd who had received
the baby, 1240 ff., and the summons to the shepherd, who was both the attend-
ant on the murdered Laius and the shepherd who, out of pity, had given the
baby away, 1215–1305). Yet these 'everyday' improbabilities only serve to accen-
tuate the completeness of Oedipus' move from total ignorance to total knowledge. The plot and its outcome follow a structure familiar to the audience –
the oracle (or dream, or other medium of prediction) which, against all probabilities and human efforts, is fulfilled in a manner not anticipated by the victim
or participants. (See, especially, the story of Adrastus in Herodotus, Book I.39–
45.)

But is that all there is? Are we meant simply to experience the virtuosity of
Sophocles' plot, or feel the anguished pity of watching foredoomed Oedipus
thrashing around in the net?

5.3 Oedipus, tragic mistakes and the gods

Prometheus, Xerxes, Antigone and Creon all came to bad ends (even if Prometheus' fate is provisional and Antigone's is self-chosen). But they do so as a result of *personal choice* (however correct/deluded). The problem with Oedipus, it would seem, is that he really has no choice about the events in his life which matter; indeed, the harder he tries to avoid the pollution, the more certainly he incurs it. He appears to make choices with all the 'philanthropy' of Prometheus and all the care for the 'unwritten laws' of Antigone, but with what result? A fate as bad as, or worse than, that of Xerxes or Creon.

Is there any sense in which Oedipus' fate has a moral dimension? In other words, is there any sense in which, like the others, he deserves – or at least controls – his fate?

Discussion _____

Those who have tried to answer 'yes' to this question cite Oedipus' behaviour during the play. He is overconfident (150ff.), suspicious and arrogant (for example, towards Tiresias, 380ff.), and tyrannical (for example, towards Creon, 594ff.) in a way that might remind us of Creon in *Antigone*. Are we looking at 'double determination' (see p.92 above)? In other words, is Oedipus' downfall simultaneously caused by the gods *and* by his own deluded arrogance and pride?

There are two problems with this view:

1   Is Oedipus really arrogant and unreasonable in the play? (His scene with Creon is the most likely evidence for this, 594ff.) Or, which is more to the point, would he have been thought so by his audience? Or is he simply acting reasonably, but as a consequence of the illusions that underlie his whole existence (for example, 645ff.)? As far as he knows, Oedipus has every reason to be certain that he has never met Laius.

2   Even if his conduct in the play is worthy of censure, surely the play does not contain 'double determination' of the kind we have seen in *The Persians*. In that play, Xerxes and the gods acted simultaneously, whereas the gods' actions with regard to Oedipus take place long before the play opens. He is for-edoomed, whatever he decides to do. ♦

Are we therefore back where we started in this section? Is Oedipus' suffering pointless? Let's look at the last part of the question above.

1   What *the play* emphasizes (as opposed to all the events referred to which happen outside it) is Oedipus' strength and determination to find out the truth, contrasted with the inactive Creon (145ff.), the reluctant Tiresias (364ff.), and the desperate Jocasta (1157ff.). He exhibits a kind of heroic stubbornness in doing what he thinks is right or necessary which we see as characteristic of Prometheus and Antigone (see Section 6.2 below). This aspect of Oedipus is explored at length in the Penguin introduction to the play (especially pp.149–52). In particular, look at the end of the play (lines 1432–end). Despite his agony, Oedipus maintains and even increases his stature (see, especially, 1586ff.); contrast the effective annihilation of Creon in *Antigone* (1420–end).

2   *The theological dimension*: as with *Antigone*, the Gods do not appear on stage, but their workings are apparent through Apollo's oracle and the appeals of the Chorus (for example, 169ff.). It is apparent that they are not reacting to human folly (Oedipus is not being punished); guilt and justice are not relevant concepts here. And, although I have counselled against relating the Theban plays too closely, it is legitimate to look at the aged Oedipus' protest of innocence in *Oedipus at Colonus* 1108ff. (p.344) and his repudiation of the idea that the gods are punishing him 'for something criminal deep inside me' (1104).

5.4 Public and private (the city and the family)

The theatre suggests two areas of human habitation – the public and the private. The public is the area of the *orchestra*, open to the view of the audience; this most prominent area is occupied by the Chorus who, in the two Sophocles plays at least (and many others), represent the city, the public domain. Contrasted with this is the private area, the area of the family, represented by what is out of sight behind the *skene*, the central door of which allows characters to pass between the two worlds.

This physical distinction reflects a tension, in the two plays of Sophocles you are reading, between public and private. In *Antigone* these two areas and the moral values they generate are represented by the conflicting and irreconcilable claims of Creon and Antigone respectively (though as is made clear above, pp.63ff., and especially Audio-Cassette 1, Band 3, this is not the whole significance of the play).

Consider for a few minutes what significance this distinction might have in Oedipus The King *(i) for the play as a whole, (ii) for Oedipus himself.*

Discussion _____

(i) The play begins and ends firmly in the public domain: what generates the plot is a plague, graphically described (14–69). The city's troubles are described in a 'ship in a storm' metaphor (29–31, 68–9) strikingly similar to *Antigone*, 179–82. (It is not irrelevant that *Oedipus The King* was probably written at about the time the Athenians experienced a real plague, at the beginning of the Peloponnesian War: Thucydides, 2.47ff.) The play ends with blinded Oedipus showing himself to the citizens of Thebes (much is made, 1430ff., of Oedipus' daring to show himself 'to the light'). Key motivating elements such as the oracle of Apollo (107ff.) and the entry of the Corinthian messenger (1012ff.) are also in the public domain. But, of course, elements crucial to the play lie offstage, in Oedipus' incestuous family. The tension in *Oedipus The King* is not between individuals representing competing claims, but within Oedipus himself.

(ii) The public and private worlds are – disastrously – combined in the character of Oedipus. Sophocles signals this verbally with the ironic ambiguity (mentioned above on p.67) at 72–3, on 'sick'. His public 'sickness' is his concern for his 'adopted' city, as its ruler; but also it is the pollution at the heart of his private life. Oedipus strives desperately to keep the action within the public domain, on the level of political corruption and conspiracy (with Tiresias and Creon), while being forced inexorably towards his private life – parricide and incest. As the play progresses, the private takes on greater and greater significance until, through the medium of the messenger speech (1365–1421), the private, domestic horror reaches the public area – the hanging of Jocasta and the blinding of Oedipus. This movement is also signalled verbally by Oedipus, with unconscious irony: his 'children' (line 1 – first words in Greek, as in the translation) are the people of Thebes but also, and more significantly, the product of his incestuous union (1599ff.). The private and the public are also related through use of the imagery of pollution in both the natural world (sowing of crops) and in sexual metaphor (lines 296, 522–3: 'he sowed the loins his father sowed'). ♦

The Chorus in this play serve to keep the public gaze trained on the central door, as it were. In concluding, I mention briefly one *stasimon* (954–997) in which the Chorus react against Jocasta's dismissal of the oracle of Apollo (948–9; see also her later abandonment of belief in the gods in favour of 'chance' – 'chance rules our lives', 1070). In this *stasimon* (the second), the Chorus express their desperate anxiety about this: if the oracle turns out to be false (which on the face of it, it was), why continue to worship the gods at all (984)? There is a need for public vindication of the gods and, in a sense, the dreadful revelation of Oedipus' family chaos reasserts divine power and authority.

5.5 Further questions

We have concentrated above on central issues. You may like to consider, or raise in a tutorial or self-help group, some of these further questions:

1 How does the Chorus function in *Oedipus The King*? Does it represent 'the audience'? (You have been given one or two pointers above; and look back at Section 2.6.1.)

2 What can be said about the other main characters in the play? Does Oedipus dominate to the extent that there is little to say about them? Or do they have distinct dramatic personalities and/or functions?

3 *Sophocles' use of language*: above we concentrated on one aspect – verbal ambiguity and dramatic irony. Consider further aspects: for example, the technique of the Messenger Speech, or the dramatic exchanges between Oedipus and Tiresias, Creon, the Corinthian messenger, or the Shepherd. What is the significance of the possibilities of three-way dialogue?

 Before you leave this section, please read the article by E.R. Dodds in The Offprints. What solutions does this offer for the problems raised in 5.2 and 5.3? And do you agree with Dodds?

5.6 Further Reading on *Oedipus the King*

DAWE, R.D. (1982) *Sophocles, Oedipus Rex*, Cambridge University Press (the standard scholarly edition, with a good introduction – especially on issues discussed in 5.2 above).

GOLDHILL, S. (1986) *Reading Greek Tragedy*, Cambridge University Press (see especially pp.205–221 on *Oedipus the King*).

KNOX, B.M.W. (1964) *The Heroic Temper: studies in Sophoclean Tragedy*, Berkeley University Press.

SEGAL, C. (1993) *Oedipus Tyrannus: tragic heroism and the limits of knowledge*, New York, Twayne's Masterwork Series, 103.

WILKINS, J. and MACLEOD, M. (1987) *Sophocles'* Antigone *and* Oedipus The King: *a companion to the Penguin translation*, Bristol Classical Press (reprinted 1994) (a useful elementary guide to both plays).

6 *PROMETHEUS BOUND, THE PERSIANS, ANTIGONE* AND *OEDIPUS THE KING*: COMPARISONS AND CONTRASTS

You have now read four Greek tragedies and have studied them in some detail. In this final section of Block 2, we are going to look back over the four plays and consider aspects of the four plays which merit further investigation, especially in terms of comparison and contrast. This section is short and, rather than attempting to round things off, it suggests lines of investigation you may like to take further on your own or in discussion. Much of what is said below is intended to point further on, to themes that will concern you subsequently in the course, in drama and elsewhere.

Please have to hand the four plays and any notes you have made while studying Sections 1–5.

6.1 Humans and gods

Prometheus Bound *and* Antigone *contain passages which celebrate the power and achievements of mortals:* Prometheus Bound *442–502 and* Antigone *377–416. Please re-read these two passages, noting similarities and watching out especially for any underlying points of contrast.*

Discussion _____

There are detailed differences between the two passages in the specific skills mentioned, but the overall pictures are similar – of humankind acquiring the necessary skills to extend its control over the environment. We noted in 2.5.2 that the *Prometheus Bound* picture of human development was essentially progressive (in comparison with Hesiod), perhaps reflecting the optimism and self-confidence of fifth-century Athens. In Block 5 we will see that the idea of the human race as largely responsible for its own development and progress towards civilization is a characteristic of one strand of philosophical thought of the second half of the fifth century associated with the sophists. In the philosophical context, this idea tends to imply a radical questioning of the traditional relationship between humans and gods. Here, we may note that *Antigone* seems to share this idea of a change in the human/divine relationship – perhaps even more so, on first sight, than *Prometheus Bound*, since the gods are not mentioned in the first three sections of *Antigone* (377–405), and humans are depicted as supreme: '...the skilled, the brilliant'.

Yet there are vital differences between the two passages. The sting in the Sophocles passage lies at the end. Humans, for all their greatness and driving ingenuity, cannot escape death and, we discover, these gifts are double-edged: they can lead to destruction as well as greatness. Humans cannot with impunity dispense with the gods and fail to harmonize human and divine concerns (406–16). The Chorus refer ostensibly to Antigone (and Polynices?) here, but there is an obvious anticipatory reference to what the gods do to Creon, later in the play, for his failure to observe the divine law. (The possible allusions in this chorus to different aspects of *Antigone* were discussed above in Section 4.5.1).

In comparison with Sophocles' vivid lyric style, Prometheus' narrative to the Chorus is more factual: the human race is also seen in a less brilliant role as a pupil under the tutelage of the 'philanthropic' god, Prometheus, who is demonstrating what he has done for mortals. Yet, in the strong emphasis on the positive relationship between humans and gods embodied in the elaborate description of how Prometheus taught the various methods of prophecy (484–98), the view of human progress in *Prometheus Bound* seems more optimistic and less fraught with the danger of humans overreaching themselves. In *Prometheus Bound*, of course, it is the god Prometheus who suffers his painful relationship with Zeus on behalf of mortals, and we have to assume that some accommodation between them was worked out in a later play of the trilogy.

That either passage had any influence on the composition of the other is highly unlikely, and we cannot be absolutely certain which came first. It is plausible to see them both as reflecting the basic idea of human progress mentioned above. But we are dealing with *drama*, and the context is all-important. The view in *Prometheus Bound* of the progress of mortals, despite their earlier narrow escape (233–4), is essentially optimistic, thanks to Prometheus, and based upon the belief that a reliable relationship can be established; it is on Prometheus himself rather than mortals that the suffering falls, as the Chorus comment immediately after his narrative (503–5). In *Antigone*, the focus is narrower, and we become aware of two things. Firstly, there is no mediator between humans and gods here: the human race, for all its power and self-confidence, is on its own. Secondly, the relationship is not an easy one. As the Chorus of elderly Thebans sing shortly before Creon's disastrous scene with his son Haemon:

> True,
> Our dreams, our high hopes voyaging far and wide

bring sheer delight to many, to many others
　　delusion, blithe mindless lusts
and the fraud steals on one slowly … unaware
till he trips and puts his foot into the fire.
　　He was a wise old man who coined
the famous saying: 'Sooner or later
foul is fair, fair is foul
to the man the gods will ruin' –
　　He goes his way for a moment only
　　　free of blinding ruin.

(lines 689–700)

You may like to consider further how 'progressive' ideas fit into the dramatic structure of their respective plays. We shall be looking at these passages from *Prometheus Bound* and *Antigone* from a different angle in Block 5.

Now, look at the other two plays. What do they add to what you have already learned from Prometheus Bound *and* Antigone?

Discussion

1　Both plays reinforce (*Oedipus The King* emphatically) the danger of being overconfident, the limitations of human knowledge and, especially, the fallacy of relying on human abilities to prosper. In *The Persians*, this is dramatized as causal progression: deluded overconfidence (Xerxes) leads to excessive behaviour which angers the gods; *Oedipus The King* on the other hand seems to emphasize the *inherent* danger facing mortals from the gods, who in *that* play are almost abstracted as 'destiny' or 'what is determined' – what is, simply, going to happen (954ff.).

2　The gods are not 'moral' or 'benevolent' (see especially Block 1, Section 3.3, paragraphs c) and d)). Their actions are seen in forms of 'trap', 'guile', 'sowing Delusion' (*The Persians*, p.125); they are also strongly motivated to love and hate (*Oedipus The King*, 902ff.). All that humans can do is to try, as best they can, to discover the gods' will and intentions through prophecy, oracles etc. (Note the temporary doubt expressed by Oedipus and Jocasta – *Oedipus The King*, 1054ff. – and their swift discovery of the truth of the oracle.)

3　The relationship is described as 'harmony' (see above, 2.5.3) or 'Justice' (*Oedipus The King*, 974ff.). This indicates – perhaps unexpectedly for the modern reader – a correct relationship between *un*equals, a recognition that there are inherent limits in what humans can achieve. And not only that; by achieving a great deal, humans risk the other extremes: pride and success turn over into ruin (*Oedipus The King*, 963–7 and see above on *Antigone*, 406 ff.). To us there may appear a clear and unbridgeable distinction between Xerxes and Oedipus in terms of responsibility and blame; the plays put more emphasis on the *process* of destruction and its effects – the *kommos* of Xerxes and the Chorus (*The Persians*, pp.147–52; *Oedipus The King*, 1433ff.). ◆

6.2　Tragedy and wrong-doing

In 4.5.2 John Purkis considered the ways in which Antigone and Creon might be considered 'tragic' characters. I would like to take this a bit further, and bring Prometheus into the discussion also.

Please read again Prometheus Bound, *1–11, 167–92, 259–70, and* Antigone, *82–113, 499–527, considering how 'willingness to compromise' and 'wrong-doing' are presented.*

Prometheus' stance is one of uncompromising defiance based both upon his conviction that he is the victim of an 'outrage' (175) and on his knowledge of the future which gives him a measure of power over his oppressor. The Chorus (176ff.) give another view: he is 'defiant' (176) and 'there is too much freedom in [his] words' (178). In 259–60 they tell him that he was wrong, a judgement which Prometheus swiftly throws back at them in 266: 'Wrong? I accept the word. I willed, willed to be wrong!'

The word which recurs throughout the play to describe Prometheus' actions is *hamartia* (error, mistake, wrong-doing), a word which reveals a wide range of meanings, from simple error ('missing the mark', literally or metaphorically) to culpable actions. It occurs with strong moral connotation in lines 8–9, in Strength's estimate of Prometheus' action as '... an offence [*hamartia*]/ Intolerable to the gods ...' resulting from ignorance, for which he must suffer and be taught better. The ambivalence of *hamartia* makes Prometheus' paradox (quoted above), 'I willed to do wrong', the more significant as a contemptuous refusal to admit that what he had done was wrong, despite apparently being almost alone in this belief.

This conviction is also a characteristic of Antigone, who (as has often been noted) shares a number of basic characteristics with Prometheus. Sophocles, like the author of *Prometheus Bound*, expresses this conviction paradoxically – for example, line 88, where the intention to defy Creon's edict and bury Polynices is described, by Antigone herself, as 'an outrage sacred to the gods' ('a righteous crime'); see also her penultimate speech (1016: 'my reverence only brands me for irreverence'). Like Prometheus, she sees the conflict in terms of honour and shame (91–2; compare *Prometheus Bound* 1038) and, like Prometheus, she is considered foolish (523–4 – but note the Sophoclean irony '... accused of folly/by a fool') and full of destructive passion (*Antigone* 962; cf. *Prometheus Bound* 1055–6).

The unwillingness of both Prometheus and Antigone to compromise is set in relief in each case by more conventional and pliable well-wishers (Oceanus, Ismene) and enemies (Hermes, Creon), whose estimate of the central character and his/her reactions to this estimate form a major strand in the texture of the plays. Yet throughout this section you will have been acutely aware of the vital differences between the two. These differences can, at least in part, be related to the general setting of the plays: *Prometheus Bound* is set in the remote past, at a time only shortly after the power struggle among the gods which resulted in the divine status quo. *Antigone*, despite its setting in Greek legend, is firmly placed in the human world, in which, in this play at least, the gods do not physically intervene, though they are a continuous background presence. (On the role of the gods in *Antigone*, see 4.5.1. above.) Prometheus is divine, and his struggle has a heroic dimension, especially in its continuous and consistent defiance of Zeus' authority. Antigone is not only mortal, but a woman; as you will remember from 4.5.3 above, her sex is a major factor contributing to her isolation and Creon's antagonism. Ismene says (74–5) 'Remember, we are women, we're not born to contend with men.'

Despite the greater isolation of Prometheus in physical terms, we are conscious of his role as the representative of unseen millions. He has a much closer and more exclusive relationship with the Chorus (see especially *Prometheus Bound* 397ff.) than Antigone, for whom Chorus sympathy comes late, just before her death (*Antigone* 895ff.). I feel we have a paradox here; Prometheus' physical loneliness is mitigated by his association with the human race (remember my discussion in 2.7.2 of the Chorus as human representatives) and his knowledge of the future. On the other hand, Antigone's isolation is claustrophobic; she is confined not only by who she is, and the inevitable restrictions on her action, but by the personal nature of her conviction. ♦

We have concentrated so far on the main character in each play. But I wonder whether you have been thinking: what about Creon? He is clearly not heroic in the Prometheus/Antigone sense; yet it is he who receives the clearest attribution of qualities we have associated with tragic characters: stubbornness, folly and pride (*Antigone* 1136–7: 'Stubbornness (*authadia*) brands you for stupidity – pride is a crime,' says Tiresias). But for Creon there is no final conviction of his own rightness; instead a total and abject confession, in lamenting the death of Haemon (1398: 'Ai, dead, lost to the world, not through your stupidity, no, my own') – where the key word, spoken by Creon, about himself, is *hamartia* (see above for definition). Creon, like Prometheus and Antigone, asserts his conviction in the face of strong opposition.

So, what is it about Creon which differentiates him from Prometheus and Antigone?

Turning to *Oedipus the King*, much has already been said about Oedipus as a tragic character; he resembles in many respects Prometheus and Antigone in his heroic resolve and determination. Yet, while the connection between tragedy and wrongdoing in *The Persians* is clear and understandable – note how the emphasis moves in this play from 'error' (p.133, ll 362ff.) to wrongdoing (Darius' speech, p.145) – the Oedipus situation is harder for us to appreciate. There is frequent talk of a 'curse' (1427, 1486, 1514, etc.). The legend suggests that Laius committed a crime (and the Athenians were familiar with curses originating with some sacrilegious act and 'inherited' by descendants, for example Pericles and the Alkmaionidai). So is Oedipus struck by the family curse? What is significant here is that Sophocles chose not to mention Laius' wrongdoing or to stress the inherited aspect of the situation (as Aeschylus did in his dramatization of the legend). It is as if Sophocles wished to focus on both the inevitability of the events and the full horror of the suffering – to 'close off', as it were, alternative explanations. Of course, having said this, we must allow that an ancient audience of *Oedipus The King* might well – from their knowledge of Aeschylus' treatment of the theme – have been much more aware than we are of Oedipus' family history.

6.3 The political dimension

In the previous sub-section, discussion of Antigone's situation suggested a parallel with Creon. In this section, I would like you to think about yet another pairing for comparison and contrast, Creon and Zeus (in *Prometheus Bound*, principally, though his function in *Antigone* is also interesting in this context). Look back at 2.7.1, starting from my question (p.33) 'How did a mid-fifth-century BCE Athenian audience react to ... the idea of Zeus as an arbitrary tyrant?' Consider once again the political terms in which Zeus' power is described. For comparison, look also at key passages of *Antigone*, such as 179–214, 566–7, 713–60. Is Creon in fact '... "the tyrant" who speaks with double tongue, praising the state while he is in fact looking for somebody to bully?' (Section 4.5.2, p.58).

To what extent can we compare and contrast these two (Zeus in Prometheus Bound *and Creon in* Antigone?*) Please think about and make your own notes on this question.*

Discussion

In Section 2.7.1, I noted the points at which Zeus' power appeared to be regarded by various participants in *Prometheus Bound* as having a degree of legitimacy. On the other hand his power is frequently called a *tyranny* not merely because it is ruthless and violent, but also because he '... keeps law within his own will' (187) and '... whose harsh and sole dominion none may call to account' (325). The idea of 'arbitrary law' feels somewhat paradoxical here, perhaps even more so in Greek, where 'law' translates *to dikaion*, with its strong connotations of 'justice'. Zeus is violent, but in one context, that of Io, this violence is also associated with sexual rapacity – a stock element in the portrayal of tyranny. (Remember how this theme was given prominence in TV1 *Seize the Fire*.) As Prometheus comments:

> Does it not seem to you that this king of the gods
> In all matters alike is given to violence?
> A god, lusting for union with this mortal maid,
> He dooms her to such journeys! [Io's wanderings]
>
> (735–8)

Finally the *newness* of Zeus' regime is continually emphasized (98, 149–52, 308–9) with the strong implication that newness = arbitrariness (as opposed to 'old and established'). ♦

What did the Athenians think about this? It must first be emphasized that, if the question is posed directly like this, no correspondingly direct answer can be given. We simply don't know what the Athenian audience thought because we have no evidence for their reactions. Yet we can make some points about political vocabulary relevant to a *probable* reaction. 'Tyrant' has a common, non-emotive use – in the context of tragic drama – to describe a ruler of, for example, mythical Thebes (*Oedipus Tyrannus* = King Oedipus). But, while in origin 'tyranny' is a term without pejorative connotations to describe personal non-constitutional rule, common in sixth-century BCE *poleis*, tyranny as a political force had strongly negative implications for later fifth-century Athenians. Athens' 'tyrant slayers', Harmodios and Aristogeiton, were *polis* heroes; Thucydides (Book 1, 122 and 124) makes the Corinthians describe Athens (twice) as a 'tyrant *polis*', and Euripides' *The Suppliants* has a strongly negative picture of rule by a dictator as opposed to 'democratic government.' More directly, rule by individuals is, by implication, contrasted with democracy by Pericles, in the Funeral Speech (Thucydides 2.37): 'Our constitution is called a democracy because power is in the hands not of a minority but of the whole people.'

It would not be an exaggeration to claim that, for the Athenians, avoidance of the exercise of personal and hence arbitrary power, was a major aim of their political system. In describing Zeus' power as 'unaccountable', Oceanus uses a political term (*euthune*: see *WA* Glossary) which describes the outgoing audit on Athenian state officials. In *Prometheus Bound*, the account of Zeus' emergence is given a strongly political flavour – he prevails, like a faction leader, in *stasis* (discord between factions within the *polis*). Tyrannical qualities – cruelty and the inability to trust anybody (222) – could be seen as part of the standard Greek view of oriental monarchies, especially those which, according to Herodotus, they had recently experienced in the Persian Wars (see especially above on *The Persians*, at Section 3.6).

It is also worth noting that the Greek word for 'new' (*kainos* and derivatives) often has the implication of 'strange', 'sinister', 'revolutionary'. So to describe Zeus' regime in these terms (for example, *Prometheus Bound*, 146–8) may well have been perceived as significant.

In *Prometheus Bound*, as Mark Griffith notes (op. cit., note on 10), Strength can refer to Zeus' tyranny with approval and nobody in the play actually ever denies the *fact* of it; but, as the play progresses, the pejorative associations of tyranny are brought out increasingly clearly.

WORDS OR EXPRESSIONS
HAVING AN UNPLEASENT
CONNOTATION.

Creon in *Antigone* also exercises absolute power, but in a very different context. He has taken the law into his own hands as an emergency measure as a result of the recent fighting between the forces of Eteocles and Polynices. His initial speech emphasizes the need to keep the 'ship of state' safe, but is belied by later developments which reveal his power as arbitrary and 'tyrannical' (Antigone on Creon, 566–7) and his belief that the city is his personal possession (in argument with Haemon, 823–5). Like Zeus in *Prometheus Bound*, he is cruel and arbitrary and his power is new.

However, contrasts between Creon in *Antigone* and Zeus in both plays, can be instructive. In *Antigone* Zeus still has absolute power, which can bring total ruin on mortals at a moment's notice (678–700) but, along with the other gods, he is the guardian of the 'unwritten laws' which Antigone unshakably opposes to Creon's edict. And it is her actions which ultimately expose Creon's real feelings and motives and lead to his downfall. Zeus the arbitrary tyrant is now also the guarantor of justice and legality.

Let's consider, for a moment, the diverse fates of Zeus and Creon. The result of Creon's actions is the destruction of his world. He assumes responsibility for the deaths of his son and wife, and all that he can wish for in his final words (1464–5) is his own death: 'Whatever I touch goes wrong – once more/a crushing fate's come down upon my head.' On the other hand, Zeus does not pay for his actions. Prometheus' threats do not come to pass and, we may assume, the conflict is in some way resolved in the later play (see above 2.7.1).

This simple and obvious contrast neatly illustrates an aspect of the Greek perception of the difference between men and gods. Absolute power, even if ultimately shorn of its more unacceptably arbitrary trappings, was an inevitable characteristic of the gods and especially their king. The audience of *Prometheus Bound* must have been aware of this, just as they were aware that similar power, exercised in a similar way by a mortal, Creon, would lead inevitably to his destruction.

Discussion of possible Athenian reaction to exercise of absolute power in the plays was also mentioned in the context of The Persians *and* Oedipus The King. *So here, finally, is a slightly different question: how far do these two plays reinforce or challenge the images that the Athenians (embodied in the audience) might have of themselves?*

Discussion _____

This is a potentially complex question, which you will need to ask again (see especially Block 4, Section 8, on Euripides' *The Women of Troy*). In the immediate context, consider these points:

1   *The Persians* (uniquely among the extant tragedies) gives the Athenians an immediate image of themselves (surely literally, in many cases, since in 472 BCE the audience would contain participants of the battles). Yet, even here, it is mediated – not just by the poet's desire to glorify the Athenians, but also by his decision to present the victory reflected, as it were, from the Persian side. So even in a 'historical' drama (and, unfortunately, we have no others for comparison) there is an invitation to the Athenians to view the events from multiple perspectives: to challenge as well as reinforce. (The historical 'myth' of the play functions not dissimilarly from other myths in Greek tragedy in this respect.)

2   *Oedipus The King*, like all other extant tragedies except *The Persians*, is based on a myth from the distant past, and belongs to a significant number of plays that explore the horror of radical disorder within the domain of the family. In this particular play the myth is loaded with significance for the Athenians – in this case the importance of maintaining a balance between intellectual, progressive and dynamic activity (celebrated by Pericles in the Funeral Speech: Thucydides, 2.34–56) and recognition of the precariousness of human existence. Oedipus functions as an *example*, not only for the Theban citizens of the Chorus (1318ff.) but also for themselves.   ♦

6.4   Conclusion

To be precise about audience reactions pushes us firmly into the realm of speculation. However, to conclude this section, I would like to leave you with one or two ideas for further consideration.

At the beginning of this block, I emphasized the placing of the plays in a physical and social context which led us to suppose that they would be concerned with matters of general importance to the *polis*. Your viewing of TV3 will give you an opportunity to look in detail at the physical context of three theatres in order to fill out my earlier sketch and use your conclusions in the study of drama later in the course. Meanwhile, for the time being, please bear in mind the following provisos:

1   The moral/political/religious commentary is not direct but mediated through the immediate subject-matter of the plays which, with only one exception – Aeschylus' *The Persians* – is taken from Greek myth and legend.

2   It follows that there is rarely *direct* proof that the Athenian audience made (or were intended to make) any specific connection between the play and political reality. We usually have to rely on probabilities. (Comedy is very different in this respect, as you will discover in Block 5.)

3   We have studied four plays, all of which are remarkable for their 'political' content. Not all *extant* tragedies (never mind the ones that do not survive – we have only 32 out of over 300 of which we know the titles!) present quite such a clear picture.

These provisos are meant to help you to exercise caution, but they should not totally stultify your imagination! We have seen that both the subject-matter and style of *Prometheus Bound, Antigone* and *Oedipus the King* reflect contemporary intellectual developments (for further discussion of which, wait for Block 5).

A further important point concerns the explicit role played by the city of Athens in the myths and legends which form the subject-matter of the plays. It is not likely to be coincidence that the tragic events never take place at Athens but in other cities, chiefly Argos, Mycenae, Thebes and Corinth, not to mention the Persian court at Susa. The effect on the Athenians of uncomfortable facts nearer home can perhaps be gauged from what happened, according to Herodotus (5.24.1) when in the wake of the fall of Miletus at the end of the Ionian Revolt (494 BCE), the playwright Phrynikos composed a tragedy on the subject: the audience burst into tears and Phrynikos was fined 1000 drachmas for reminding the Athenians of their 'domestic ills' (Miletus was an Ionian city founded, according to tradition, from Athens). On the other hand, legendary Athens does feature explicitly in a number of tragedies as a supporter of justice against injustice and the city is the subject of a number of complimentary references in choral odes.

Direct references to Athens are usually complimentary (except where uncomplimentary remarks are made by characters clearly established in the dramatic context as 'baddies'). Such passages imply (or even directly state) support, projected back into the legendary past, for the Athenian political system, its values and institutions (see especially *ST* 11(a)). The legendary Athenian king Theseus is invariably made the mouthpiece of popular sentiment (just as Creon, the Theban, is out of tune with it). Can we say, then, that there is a self-congratulatory, even jingoistic element in Greek tragedy? Or is it possible that the absence of *direct* reference enabled the Athenians indirectly to receive and accept important, and not necessarily bland or consoling, truths about themselves and their existence? You will have an opportunity to consider this idea further, especially in Blocks 4 and 5, where you will be able to read two further tragic dramas, by the third of our trio of playwrights, Euripides, and also a comedy by Aristophanes.

6.5   Further Reading on tragedy in general

For bibliography specifically related to the four plays, see 2.8, 3.8, 4.6 and 5.6.

1   On the historical and ceremonial background to the performance of drama, the standard work is:

PICKARD-CAMBRIDGE, A. (1988, 2nd edn) *The Dramatic Festivals of Athens*, revised by J. Gould and D.M. Lewis, Oxford, Oxford University Press; especially Chapter 2.

The actual design of the fifth-century theatre (a topic covered extensively in TV3) is discussed in another work by Pickard-Cambridge: *The Theatre of Dionysos at Athens* (Oxford, Oxford University Press, 1956), Chapters I–III on the 'Periclean theatre'. In some respects this is now archaeologically out of date (the 'Periclean theatre' of P-C turns out to be fourth-century BCE) and can be supplemented with the short, readable and authoritative *The Ancient Theatre* by E. Simon, translated from German by C.E. Vafopoulou-Richardson (London, Methuen, 1982).

Although these are both specialist books, they might be found in a large public library (especially Simon).

2   There are two short and approachable books on the practical and dramatic aspects of Greek tragedy:

   a)   TAPLIN, O. (1978) *Greek Tragedy in Action*, London, Methuen; available in paperback. Unlike *Stagecraft in Aeschylus*, this one is short and designed for beginners.

   b)   WALTON, J.M. (1984) *The Greek Sense of the Theatre; Tragedy Reviewed*, London, Methuen; a useful compendium of advice on the staging and visual dimension of the plays.

3   Three books which discuss Greek tragedy in general are:

   a)   GREEN, J.R. (1994) *Theatre in Ancient Greek Society*, London and New York, Routledge.

   b)   VICKERS, B. (1973) *Towards Greek Tragedy*, London, Longman; long, but very stimulating analysis of Greek tragedy, concentrating on the texts themselves (good sections on *Prometheus Bound* and *Antigone* – use the *Index*, but don't fail to read the first chapter also).

   c)   WALCOT, P. (1976) *Greek Drama in its Theatrical and Social Context*, Cardiff, University of Wales Press; paperback. A short book which contains an incisive account of the Greek theatre and its background.

4   LEFKOWITZ, M. (1981) *The Lives of the Greek Poets*, London, Duckworth; analyses the evidence for the biographical 'facts' handed down to us (including tragedians).

5   Finally, on Greek tragedy as a 'theatre of ideas', see the contrasted approaches of:

   a)   GOLDHILL, S. (1986) *Reading Greek Tragedy*, Cambridge, Cambridge University Press; paperback. Looks at ideas underlying tension and conflict in Greek tragedy; a stimulating book (already quoted in connexion with *Antigone*), which reflects some of the ideas of literary critical studies and linguistic analysis.

   b)   HEATH, M. (1987) *The Poetics of Greek Tragedy*, Oxford, Oxford University Press; concerned to argue the thesis (by implication rejected in this block) that Greek tragedians were not primarily concerned with political or social ideas.

Both Goldhill and Heath are stimulating but dense; it is recommended that you try, for example, Walcot or Taplin first.

Finally, on Homer and Greek tragedy, you should listen to Band 1 of Cassette 9, a Guest Lecture by Oliver Taplin.

Appendix 1: Outline map of the Eastern Mediterranean, showing places mentioned in Block 1

(You might like to mark in other important places as your work progresses.)

Mykale
Miletos
IONIA
Samos
Hellespont
Delos
Thasos
AEGEAN SEA
Marathon
Athens
Plataia
ATTICA
Salamis
Artemision
Thermopylai
Isthmus
Corinth
Delphi
PELOPONNESE
Sparta
Olympia
MEDITERRANEAN SEA

0   50   100 km